Rediscovering LEADERSHIP

Essential Principles for Successful Leadership

Kirimi Barine

Praise for Rediscovering Leadership

Kirimi Barine has captured the essence of effective leadership. His own experience and study makes his message relevant and fresh for leaders in any area of life. He has bridged the biblical message into the world of business and education. He leads all who read his book to the model servant leader of all time, Jesus Christ. I recommend this book for both the student and practitioner of leadership.

C. Gene Wilkes, Ph.D.
Author - Jesus On Leadership
U.S.A.

Do you desire to be a powerful and courageous leader, full of godly character and mightily used by God? Do you have a passion to fulfill the leadership call that God has on your life? You will want to buy this book. In *Rediscovering Leadership: Essential Principles for Successful Leadership,* Barine brings a fresh look at leadership and shares some insightful principles that will positively affect your thoughts about leadership. Leadership is not a onetime goal to be attained, but as Barine suggests, leadership is a process. To be an effective leader a person must make it his or her goal to continue learning how to lead. The material contained in this book will assist you in that process of learning.

Richard Brott
Executive Director at ABC Book Publishing, L.L.C.
Oregon, U.S.A.

The content of this book has had a life changing effect on my leadership concept and practice. *Rediscovering Leadership* does not offer theories and hypothesis of leadership concepts. It is written from biblical and practical principles that have potential to revolutionize the present and future leadership within the church and society in general. This book is one of the few in the market, armed with well researched practical facts that will unlock the leadership potential in every person who reads it. This is a must read book for all leaders who wish to have a clear and well articulated biblical perspective of leadership.

Rev. Stephen K. Barine
African Ministry Pastor, Crossroads Fellowship Church
North Carolina, U.S.A.

In every science experiment, the results must be replicated in order for the conclusion drawn to be considered true. Barine has experimented with leadership in his own life and concluded, leading many and setting the godly example in servant leadership that all leaders must attain. It is my hope and expectation that each reader of *Rediscovering Leadership* will be the replication of this experiment and the concluding principles shall be found true.

Trevor Buelor
Canada

The challenge for any leader is to understand leadership. Africa has many leaders who have a distorted approach to this challenge. Kirimi Barine clearly understands the African problem and identifies crucial biblical principles to help us be successful in our leadership. This is an inspirational work by an African author who gives a 'human face' to his leadership journey and insight.

David Kadalie
Author – Leader's Resource Kit
South Africa

It's only somebody who has had the experience in leadership that could prepare such special material about this subject. In this book, Barine has given us a clear way to understand the leader's environment – the calling, challenges, conflicts, need of preparation, values, principles, and the key: dependence of God. Combining the most important principles about leadership that we can find around the world with biblical examples, this book can help us to increase our leadership practice. Only a person who lives those values in his or her day-to-day leadership, and seeks God's direction for his decision can give to us such a special gift.

Pastor Davidson Freitas

Brazil

This book is a treasure house of hard facts about leadership. It will be of tremendous help to both the upcoming and the veteran leader alike. Not only does it speak to the mind, but it reaches to the depths of our hearts and souls.

Rev. Nick Mbai

Nairobi, Kenya

My friend Barine raises a fundamental question in his book, "is our world's crisis today driven from a lack of leadership?" I contest that it is true not only for the world but also in the church where godly leaders are needed. I recommend this great book to anyone who leads or follows.

Pastor Ayad Bebawy

Egypt

There are not as many writers who have written a book on leadership in such a detailed and practical way as Kirimi Barine has done. The book is an expression of his heart and passion for leadership. I encourage you to read this book and your leadership will not be the same again.

Kusnadi Kunawi

Jakarta, Indonesia

Every now and then The Lord will use someone, circumstances or a book to bring our focus back to Him. As I read *Rediscovering Leadership: Essential Principles for With Successful Leadership* by Kirimi Barine, I recognized God's Hand in using this book to bring me back to the calling He had placed on my life. I had to cast the shackles of mechanicalism, mediocrity and self-reliance and come back to The One who Calls and Equips. This book served as a wake up call and prescription to get my spiritual health back on track.

Daniel Scott Mays

Australia

I always thought that Leadership was for the people who had titles and that the rest of the people had nothing to do with it. This book, Rediscovering Leadership, has served to stitch in my mind that leadership is for every person. After all, every one of us is to lead ourselves if not our families. The book shows the value of leadership in its smaller context (the family) and wires how it affects the church, organizations and the state. I have finally reconciled my thoughts that leadership is for me after going through the well-crafted examples of the book based on the biblical heroes of leadership. God bless Kirimi Barine to write more and more to provide timely and gap filling insights.

Hermela Solomon

Addis Ababa, Ethiopia

Barine's choice of title for this book "Rediscovering Leadership" is spot on! The book is equally appropriate and timely. The book addresses the need to grow other leaders, which is a great leadership pitfall for many leaders today. The book is written from years of personal experience in leadership and his observations of leaders in the religious, corporate and public sectors. Barine has built on the biblical foundations and has many insightful, practical and relevant principles. It is a guide for anyone who wants to be an effective leader and who is also growing other effective leaders. In many ways, it is an A to Z book on leadership.

Rev. Elijah Wanje,

Senior Pastor, Ridgeways Baptist Church,

Nairobi, Kenya

Rediscovering LEADERSHIP

Essential Principles for Successful Leadership

Rediscovering Leadership: Essential Principles for Successful Leadership

© Copyright 2013 by KIRIMI BARINE
Revised and Updated Edition 2015
All Rights Reserved

Published by

P.O. Box 58411,
Releigh, NC 27658
U.S.A.
info@integritypublishers.org
www. info@integritypublishers.org

ISBN: 978-1-93745 5-28-6

Publishing Consultants:

P.O. Box 16458 – 00100
NAIROBI
KENYA
info@publishing-institute.org
www.publishing-institute.org

First published as Rediscovering Leadership: Principles to Launch and Grow Your Leadership in 2007 by Lifespring International, Nairobi, Kenya.

All Scripture quotations, unless otherwise indicated, are taken from the Holy Bible, New International Version ®. NIV ®. Copyright © 1973, 1978, 1984 by International Bible Society. Used by permission of Zondervan Publishing House. All rights reserved.

All rights reserved, including the right to reproduce this book, or any portions thereof, in any form. No part of this book may be reproduced or transmitted in any form or by any other means, electronic or mechanical, magnetic, chemical, optical, manual, or otherwise, including photocopying, recording, or by any information storage or retrieval system without written permission from the author. All rights for publishing this book or portions thereof in other languages are contracted by the author.

Every effort has been made to supply complete and accurate information. However, neither the publisher nor the author assumes any responsibility for its use, nor any infringements of patents or other rights of third parties that would result.

Printed in U.S.A.

CONTENTS

Acknowledgements · xi
Foreword · xiii
Preface · xvii

PART ONE: THE BASICS

1. The Leadership Challenge · 3
2. Understanding Leadership · 13

PART TWO: THE PRINCIPLES

3. Leadership is a Calling · 29
4. Leadership Requires Preparation · 49
5. Leadership is Character · 61
6. Successful Leaders Depend on God · 71
7. Leadership Requires Courage · 83
8. Leaders Experience Conflict · 103
9. Leadership Requires Communication · 111
10. Age is Just but a Number · 119

PART THREE: WHAT NEXT?

11. Leadership: Your Responsibility · 137
12. Epilogue: Fulfill Your Leadership · 143

Dedicated to:

To all Leaders whose desire is to make a difference where God has called them by modelling servant leadership

and

To my departed dad – Rev. Phinehas Barine from whom I saw some of the principles shared in this book applied first hand. He made me appreciate that my labour in the Lord is not in vain.

ACKNOWLEDGEMENTS

I cannot claim to have written this book alone. There are many people whom God has placed in my path of life who have greatly encouraged and enriched me, added great value to my life and have a great joy to be with.

On top of this list is my wife, Joyce and our two lovely sons, Alvin and Adrian. You have stood with me at all times even when I have had to learn the most painful lessons on leadership. You have shared in my successes but at the same time had to contend with my faults and failures.

I grew up in a family where I was taught the fear of the Lord, which is the spring of all wisdom. My parents and my siblings have been an encouragement. To Stephen and Mary Barine, I have been encouraged and challenged by your dedication to serve God wherever and whenever he sends you.

I will be eternally grateful for the many fine servant leaders God has placed in my life. The list of these is so long that I dare not name one for I have no space to recognize you all. The lessons in this book would not have been possible without you all.

I have had a privilege of serving in great institutions that enriched my leadership experience. Starting with my local church, Kahawa Sukari Baptist Church where I have served in various leadership capacities and in Pan Africa Christian University as well as Evangel Publishing House among others. I appreciate all those who believed in my leadership before testing. Blessed are you who believe without seeing for through your faith, my leadership potential was discovered. Kirk Kauffeldt and

Wilf Hilderbradnt contributed greatly to this journey of self-discovery while at PAC University.

I have had the privilege of meeting and discussing leadership issues with government, business, church and community leaders from around the world. These have added new perspectives and understanding of leadership of which I am glad to share the experiences.

As the saying goes, good writing is good rewriting. In the process of rewriting my manuscript and later with the updated version, I have had the support and encouragement of dear friends. To Esther, Macharia and Catherine, you were part of the writing of this book and you deserve recognition.

Since this book is a by product of my interactions with people, events and circumstances over my lifetime, I would need so much space to mention every person who has contributed to this book. For those who have sent an email or called to share how the earlier edition of this book encouraged you, I say thank you so much. I appreciate that the truths shared have and will continue to impact lives and inspire the desire to model servant leadership as Jesus did.

FOREWORD

Leaders must always be continuous learners for if they stop learning today, they will stop leading effectively tomorrow. There is no graduation ceremony for leaders because their education never ends. They have a never ending thirst for learning more about how to lead. Gaps in understanding must always be filled in through more knowledge, skill acquisition and application. Even when a gap is filled, however, it requires fine tuning to meet the needs of changing circumstances and the challenges of working with different personalities. The road to successful leadership is often full of landmines, potholes, and detours placed in the way by unsuspecting, ignorant, or malicious people along the journey. Why do some people cheer while others whine? Why are some easily moved while others are immobile? Why do some grasp and run with an idea while others see only road blocks? To find out, the leader must look beyond the smiles or frowns to what is in a person's heart. Character and attitude are as important as skills and experiences. Yet it is the cooperation of these very people that a leader is dependent upon to make his or her plans a reality through the application of sound leadership principles. That is why getting the leadership principles found in this book right in the first place is so important. Leaders do not exist to produce followers, but other leaders who will carry on after them. By mastering and demonstrating the validity of these principles in their leadership, they can pass them on to other leaders. True leaders are always more concerned with developing what someone can be than what they currently are.

There have been literally thousands of recent books published on leadership and about leaders. Instead of being bored by the subject, we are inextricably drawn to look for yet more clues on how to define, explain and develop future leaders for the family, church, community, society, and nation. The confusion that exists around what leadership really is can be found in the widespread collection of definitions found at the end of this book. Even those people who cannot explain what a leader is or does, can tell a good leader from a bad one when they see and sometimes experience them in action. The point is that there will never be enough good books on leadership because each one introduces perspectives from the eyes and experiences of yet another leader in a different context and set of circumstances. Every great event in human history, however small or large, was a result of leadership that calls forth a re-examination of those who led, such as New York Mayor Rudolph Guilliani after his experiences in the 9/11 terrorist attacks on the World Trade Center, Billy Graham after his crusades, Bill Clinton after his two terms as US president, and Bill Gates on making Microsoft the giant in the software business. They serve to keep us in tune with basic leadership principles and lessons that too many leaders so easily forget when exercising their leadership responsibilities. Still, there is so much more to learn about leaders and *Rediscovering Leadership* brings us back to fundamental principles that must be applied in all forms of leadership, and especially by those who seek to lead based on biblical principles.

In today's world, so many leaders in politics, business, church, education, government, and the not-for-profit and voluntary sectors have lost their way because they have not adhered to the God-ordained foundations for good leadership. Aspiring or developing leaders are uncertain of the right path to take because they are missing important signposts to lead them there. Too many people today still see the leader as the person at the top of an organization who has all of the perks, privileges, and power, when in reality the real leader is at the bottom of the organizational pyramid. It is the leader who bears responsibility for their followers, not vice versa. It is the leader who makes the tough decisions in the interests of followers whom they are called to serve. While knowledge, competence, skills, and intelligence are important attributes of a leader, truly great leaders have a solid faith in God that enables them to feel accepted and loved and to find a way forward when, in human terms, one does not seem to exist. They move forward on their knees, not their bravado.

A key reason why some organizations move forward and others do not is found in their honesty and integrity. In either case, it is because their leaders have set the tone through their identification and practice of core principles. Leaders can never expect their organization to exemplify principles that they do not themselves espouse and follow religiously. The character of a leader becomes the character of the group. If winning at all costs is all that matters, then that philosophy will be reflected in the organization's values and ethics. If honoring God is at the philosophical centre of the organization, then His word will be the basis for all decisions. Leaders must be held responsible for making sure that the moral compass of their organization is set in the right direction.

There are many good things that Christian leaders can do, but it should only be God-things that they actually do. Christian leaders are called to discern between what may be good in their own eyes but not in God's eyes and vice versa with the result that in doing God's will they will uplift those around them. Barine reminds us how important it is to ensure that our leadership is intimately connected to the leading of the Holy Spirit in our lives. Is our leadership meant to serve ourselves or God? The most important quality that God wants to see in leaders is a dependence on Him first and foremost. When leaders make decisions based on their own reason and analysis or to please others instead of being led by the Holy Spirit, they are severing their dependence upon God or, as Ken Blanchard has said, they are letting their own egos get in the way by Edging God Out. That is why in Rediscovering Leadership, Barine is asking leaders to ask God to show them the way. To do so, leaders must remember that the B-I-B-L-E is God's direction for bringing to us Basic Instructions Bringing Leadership Excellence.

Rediscovering Leadership isn't about showing people how energetic or vision-driven you are, it's about gaining enough knowledge and wisdom to influence people to move in a godly direction that is for their collective benefit.

Barine's proven principles are for finding your way through the maze of uncertain times to a better future for any organization that is based on the quality of its leadership. *Rediscovering Leadership* is filled with gems of wisdom drawn from Barine's own experiences in leadership and as a teacher and observer of leaders, from insightful, motivational, and memorable quotations from some of his favorite authors and thinkers on leadership, and pertinent biblical insights. These poignant quotations are skillfully interwoven through the text so that the reader will understand the forcefulness of his arguments and be inspired to unlock the hidden potential that everyone has to be a better leader. Not only will leaders themselves benefit from this transformation, but the impact of this kind of godly leadership will be felt by those whom the leader serves. For some leaders, his points may appear as strong medicine for spiritually rejuvenating a decaying society, only to find that the cure is worth the prescription.

Each chapter ends with thoughtful action points that will cause all those who aspire to lead to reflect on their leadership. The authenticity of this book is based on the author's passion to walk with and serve God with humility and truth. This comes through spiritual connections on page after page. Putting it into a leadership context, Matthew 5:16 might read: Let your accomplishments, processes, and relationships so shine before others that they may see your good leadership through which you glorify your heavenly Father. And, in Barine's own words, apply these principles with commitment, consistency, and credibility. That is and has always been the heart of successful godly leadership.

DON PAGE
PROFESSOR OF LEADERSHIP STUDIES
TRINITY WESTERN UNIVERSITY – CANADA

PREFACE

Every leader experiences diverse challenges in their leadership journey from time to time. This book is meant to re-energize those in leadership and to inspire those thinking about accepting leadership roles. It will take you back to the basics of successful leadership. In addition, it will also remind you of the biblical principles that have been used over time so that you can safely grow your leadership capacity to the highest level possible. It is a great tool to help you navigate through the diverse challenges that any leader experiences in their leadership journey.

These principles have been taken mainly from the first chapter of the Book of Jeremiah. Here, we read of God's call to Jeremiah to be his prophet. God makes it clear to Jeremiah that despite his insufficiency (i.e. his young age, the negative attitude of the people he was to serve, among others) his calling was sufficient for the task. God promised to go with Jeremiah, assuring him of His presence and security. Therefore, Jeremiah had no reason to be afraid.

My prayer is that as you flip through these pages, you will be encouraged to pursue your calling to leadership.

Barine

Part One

The Basics

1

THE LEADERSHIP CHALLENGE

Recently, a friend recommended that I read a book he had enjoyed reading on the subject of leadership. Having known my interest in the study of leadership, he knew that I would find "Too many Bosses, Too few Leaders" by Rajeev Peshawaria a useful read. The sub title of the book: "The three essential principles you need to become an extraordinary leader" created the impression that in all spheres of life, there are ordinary and extraordinary leaders. What was more striking from my reading however was an assertion by the author in his introduction. He states that as a leadership and management consultant and educator, there is a question he poses to the thousands of business executives in every continent across a wide range of industries to both seniors at the twilight of their careers as well as upcoming middle managers, "Of all the bosses you have had in your career, how many would you call truly great leaders? For the purpose of this question, a great leader is one who inspired you to show up every morning and do your best possible work, someone who made you believe in yourself, someone who genuinely cared about your success and someone who you wanted to follow willingly." Rajeev opines that regardless of context, geography or cultural differences, the average answer in any group lies somewhere between zero and two. His conclusion; this is baffling given the abundance of research and literature on the subject of leadership as well as the sums invested by organizations every year on leadership development. If you keenly look at the society that we are living in today, you will realize that leadership is one of the challenges we have to deal with. There are so many leaders yet there still seems to be little if any leadership at all.

The above statement does not in any way suggest a power vacuum. The statement reflects a leadership that is not keeping with the times we are in; one that has failed to foresee, shape and plan the future. We are experiencing a lack of leaders who will provide effective leadership in the face of changing paradigms.

LEADERSHIP IN THE FAMILY

The sermon delivered at our wedding day ceremony still remains vivid in my mind. When the pastor took to the podium, the message of the day was the need for men to provide leadership in their homes. The premise of his argument was on the biblical truth that the man is the head of his home according to Ephesians 5:23. To illustrate his point further, the pastor explained that if you came across a mad man, it will be very clear that that man doesn't have a problem with his hand, leg or stomach; his main problem would be traced back to his head. In the same manner as he explained, if you come across a dysfunctional family, then definitely the problem could easily be traced to the head of that family, in this case the man.

The family is the basic foundation on which all leadership is experienced. It's at the family level that we first encounter functional or dysfunctional leadership. When Paul gave advice to the young Timothy on the qualifications for church leadership, he said that *"He must manage his own family well and see that his children obey him with proper respect" (1 Timothy 3:4)*. The rationale behind this requirement is that if one cannot take care of a small unit like the family, how can they take care of God's church?

A survey of the family unit around the world gives a picture of a struggling unit. The struggle is to keep its head above the waters threatening to sink it and provide the very basis for leadership as is expected.

THE LEADERSHIP CHALLENGE

The family is the basic foundation on which all leadership is launched. It's at the family level that we first encounter functional or dysfunctional leadership.

According to the United Nations World Top 10 highest divorce rate (2011) based on the sum of average male & average female divorce rates, Latvia leads with a divorce rate of 27.96, followed by Czech Republic and Lithuania with 24.26 and 24.08 respectively. From my observation, I am convinced that the increasing rate of divorce worldwide originates from leadership challenge in the family unit among other contributing factors. As a result of divorce, children grow up in families that do not model the kind of leadership that they need to embody. It is needful to note that this is not a theory but a hypothesis. The lack of leadership in the family spills over into our institutions and the communities we live in. This is because children who grow up in families where leadership is dysfunctional, exercise the same kind of leadership they have experienced when presented with an opportunity in the corporate, church or community level. If we are to change bad leadership, it is expedient that we must begin at the family unit.

If leadership is functional in the home, children learn the art of consultation, team work, conflict resolution and communication among other virtues. In its absence, the opposite is experienced.

A survey conducted by the author on a group of young families ranging between the ages of 25 – 40 years on some of the leadership challenges they faced in their families, identified the following as some of the root causes of bad leadership in families:

- Men assuming the 'alpha and omega' position in all decision making and determining the destiny of the family, without consultation or involvement of their spouse and children. Children never get to experience a model of leadership where communication, consultation and mutual respect is practiced.

- Parents who are never there to model good leadership to their children. This in turn leaves their children to model what they see on television or what their school teachers and caregivers offer, whether good or bad.

- Conflicting expectations between parents and children. This conflict is often as a result of poor communication.

The Blackabys in *Spiritual Leadership* state that wise leaders strive to preserve their families in the midst of the pressures on their professional lives. Most leaders love their families, but many fail to apply the same prioritizing skills they use at work when relating to the most important people in their lives. Leaders must be proactive as they respond to their God-given responsibilities for their families. They further add that there is an exigent nature to leader's family (Deut. 6:4-9). Their children represent the future generation of leaders. Emerging leaders at home have potential to impact the world even more that their parents did. It is imperative for today's leaders to help their children develop as Christians and as the next generation of leaders.

LEADERSHIP IN THE CHURCH

The leadership challenge is not confined to the family unit alone, but is evident in the church as well. Unlike the first New Testament church that turned the world upside down in less than a century, today's church falls short of expectations in fulfilling the mandate given to it by the Lord.

> *But when they did not find them, they dragged Jason and some other brothers before the city officials, shouting: 'these men who have caused trouble all over the world have now come here' (Acts 17:6).*

As church leaders jostle for power and control, the institution that is supposed to be a beacon of tranquility has come to be associated with moral decadence and court battles that at times degenerate into open fights where blood has been shed. Resources that members give for the expansion of the kingdom are sometimes misdirected and used to purchase status symbols (like big cars) to demonstrate "blessedness" of the ministry. This statement however should not be construed to mean that I am opposed to the good treatment of ministers.

The management style practiced by the early church was characterized by openness and is evidenced by the fact that members were willing to sell their property and bring proceeds at the apostles' feet who shared according to the needs of all. Further, it is evident that the apostles' did not use these resources for self gain from the fact that these church leaders continued to be people of meager resources. Indeed when Peter and John were asked for alms by the disabled person at Gate Beautiful, their response was, "*Silver and gold have we none . . .* " (Acts 3:6) an indication of their lack of money.

> *The management style practiced by the early church was characterized by openness and is evidenced by the fact that members were willing to sell their property and bring proceeds at the apostles' feet who shared according to the needs of all.*

Today, we are confronted with many leaders who cannot stand the test of integrity; leaders who are so secretive that they manage church funds from their pockets and are also fearful of relinquishing power that they will not hesitate to encourage party spirit as they rally loyal members for support. Such leaders do not even delegate responsibility for fear that other people will prove to be better than they are and thus threaten their position. If they must delegate responsibility -on account of sickness, for instance, - they make sure that authority remains with them. The effect of all this, has been a church that is ill-prepared in influencing society with the gospel. The church has failed in its primary role of being the light and the salt of the earth. All is not lost though, it is possible to change today's sorry state of church leadership and introduce new impetus that will enable it to continue fulfilling its God - given mandate.

LEADERSHIP IN THE CORPORATE SCENE

If you observe our society carefully, you will find out that most institutions are characterized by either bad or poor leadership, or worse still, lack of leadership. These institutions are on the verge of collapse if they have not collapsed already. Such institutions' performance can be greatly enhanced if only good leadership is provided.

The effect of bad, poor or no leadership has had a toll on the corporate scene. For many centuries, Switzerland was the world leader in watch making. In 1967, during a watch Manufactures' forum, a Swiss engineer suggested the possibility of producing electronic watches. Swiss industry leaders, for lack of vision, gave the idea a cold shoulder. A Japanese engineer however overheard the suggestion and leaked it to his people who implemented it immediately; this as you may know changed the market leadership in the watch industry.

A similar case was repeated in 1973 when the oil crisis set in and European vehicle manufacturers were caught unprepared. The Japanese, who had anticipated the new developments, came up with small low-consumption vehicles and assumed leadership in that field as well.

The case of Enron cannot be left out in the discussion of bad, poor or absence of leadership in the corporate scene. Enron Corporation was an American energy company based in Houston, Texas. Before its bankruptcy in late 2001, Enron employed around 21,000 people and was one of the world's leading electricity, natural gas, pulp and paper, and communications companies, with claimed revenues of $111 billion in 2000(McLean & Elkind, 2003). *Fortune* named Enron "America's Most Innovative Company" for six consecutive years. At the end of 2001, it achieved infamy, when it was revealed that its reported financial condition was sustained mostly by institutionalized, systematic, and creatively planned accounting fraud. The scandal caused Enron's downfall and the dissolution of the Arthur Andersen accounting firm.

Examples of challenges I have found in institutional leadership include leaders who:

- Lack integrity and very often compromise to sustain the notion that profit must keep rising from year to year.

- Lack understanding of the value or respect for established structures that are supposed to improve decision-making and governance.

- Struggle to delegate and when they do so, only delegate responsibility and not authority.

- Lack understanding of the difference between policy making and policy implementation in organizations. In other words leaders who keep on meddling into things that others should be doing or spend their time campaigning to win support from board members even for ideas that have no merit.

- Fail to appreciate the dynamism in the society and hence fail to accept the changing times. This results in leaders who maintain a conventional stand on issues and claim that 'we have always done things this way'.

- Harbour the erroneous thought that they have been mandated to be served rather than serve. As a result, they do not look for opportunities to serve others but seek for every opportunity to be served.

- Disregard other people's opinions and think they know it all.

LEADERSHIP IN THE POLITICAL SCENE

Apparently, the leadership challenge is also evident in the political arena as well. Many African countries have celebrated half a century since they became independent, yet the continent continues to lag behind in a host of ways. Despite having all manner of natural resources and farmlands, people continue to be ravaged by disease, hunger and poverty. This has largely been due to the absence of good leadership that is sensitive to the needs of the people.

In Kenya for example, some of the challenges witnessed in the political leadership include:

- Leaders who rally groups to support them whether the agenda and policies they hold for the society are favourable or not. This is indeed the height of selfishness where the drive is more on individual gain than the well being of the society.

- Leaders who propagate lies to gain political mileage over their opponents.

Despite having all manner of natural resources and farmlands, people continue to be ravaged by disease, hunger and poverty. This has largely been due to the absence of good leadership that is sensitive to the needs of the people.

If we are to make a difference in the society we live in, we must rise above the leadership practices evident today. For us to do this, we need to understand some basic principles that will help us escalate the ladder as far as our leadership practice is concerned. These are the principles shared in this book.

We need to develop an attitude like that of Apostle Paul and declare that "I can do all things through Him who gives me the strength." We must admit that we can lead differently through Christ's enabling power in our lives.

Some of the challenges we will have to contend with include:

- Leading in a changing world – societal values, technological, economical, political and environmental changes are taking place all the time.

- People like to be called or referred to as leaders but the greatest challenge is if they can rise to the occasion and provide the necessary leadership. In many African communities for instance, the term leader is still regarded as a value laden title that accords one many privileges and opportunities. This explains why people will jostle for leadership at any given opportunity.

- Leading by serving as opposed to being served.

- Leading in a world that no longer regards boundaries. Day after day, we are talking about the world turning into a global village and the effects and changes are enormous.

- Adopting a learning attitude to overcome these and many other challenges we may experience.

Another great challenge that I find in today's leadership is derived from the advice that was given to Moses by Jethro (his father-in-law). Jethro, together with Zipporah, Moses' wife and his two sons (Gersom and Eliezer) had gone to visit Moses in the wilderness at the mountain of God where Moses had encamped. They found out that Moses had a duty of sitting down to judge the Israelites from morning till evening everyday. Jethro was alarmed by such an exercise and recommended to Moses to delegate his responsibility of judging the people to men whose criteria of selection would be based on ability, fear for God, truthfulness and those who hate covetousness. These men were to be placed over thousands, hundreds, fifties and tens. From this conversation, we discover that we have particular leaders whose responsibility and ability is wired for leading ten people and so giving them leadership over hundreds will prove to be disastrous. It is definite that because of their capacity, you will be setting them up for failure. In the same manner, if we let the leaders meant to lead thousands only lead tens, then undoubtedly they will be under utilized and either scenario does not yield optimum results.

To overcome these challenges, Barbara Kellerman has several guidelines that will be helpful to both leaders and followers and are found in chapter eleven on *Leadership: Your responsibility.*

The onus is on us to be focused in our leadership and declare that we will be different irrespective of the kind of leadership around us.

I wish you the very best.

PRAYER FOR THE LEADER

Father, we have experienced the deficiency of leadership in our families, churches, corporations and communities. I pray that you may raise men and women who will fill in the gaps where they may exist. Empower those whom you have called to lead. Help us to identify and deal with challenges that may pose a threat to leadership in our circles of influence. We ask this in Jesus' name.
Amen.

STOP: CHECK POINT

1. What are some of the leadership challenges that you can identify in your current environment?
2. How can you overcome these challenges?

2

UNDERSTANDING LEADERSHIP

Many who aspire to leadership fail because they've never learned to follow. They are like boys playing war in the street, but all is quiet. When you ask," Is there a truce?" They respond, "No, we are all generals. No one will obey the command to charge.

J. OSWALD SANDERS

God blessed them: 'Prosper! Reproduce! Fill earth! Take Charge! Be responsible . . . Genesis 1:28 (Message)

A chinese proverb says that if you think you are leading and there is no one following, then you are simply taking a walk. One does not become a leader because of the position that they hold in the group but rather because of their ability to galvanize the group and rally it to a common cause.

My quest to understand leadership dates back to the time when I was a young boy. One day, I accompanied my mother to the consecration service of a Presbyterian clergy. Although I did not quite understand the significance of everything that was taking place, a song that was sang during the occasion captured my attention. That song's literal translation goes like this, "He who is holy and consecrated to God was presented before the congregation for them to know and affirm that he had been set apart for leadership." As we walked home and for a couple of days that followed, I asked my mother many questions about that occasion.

As a result of the content of the song, I began to question why people choose to revolt against leaders if and when they know that God has set them apart for leadership. Since I could not get satisfactory answers to these questions, I began to read any material on leadership that I lay my hand on, in an effort to understand this very interesting aspect of human behavior.

The book of Genesis unfolds the record of the beginning of the world and of human history. In Genesis 1:27-28, God blessed Adam and Eve and commanded them, *'Prosper! Reproduce! Fill earth! Take Charge! Be Responsible.'* (Message) From this command, we can conclude that leadership is as old as mankind. However, if we look at the family, church, government, or corporate organizations, the issue of leadership remains a great challenge. This is because our natural expectation is that man would have mastered leadership and developed it in the same way he has done with technology.

In the book of Genis, the Bible records,

So God created man in his own image, in the image of God he created him; male and female he created them. God blessed them and said to them, 'Be fruitful and increase in number; fill the earth and subdue it. Rule over the fish of the sea and the birds of the air and over every living creature that moves on the ground. (Genesis 1:27-28)

When God created man, He had a plan for him; to lead His creation. This simply means that God handed the leadership baton to man. This implies that God was and still is the Master Leader and only wanted Adam to take the cue from Him. One of the reasons why godly leadership is missing in our society today can be attributed to the fact that our leaders do not take the cue from God as they seek to develop and grow their leadership.

Two profound leadership lessons that we learn from the creation story in Genesis are:
- God by nature is a Leader and He created us in His image (in the same way) to be leaders. That is why the scripture says: "God created

human beings; he created *them godlike, reflecting God's nature . ..."* *(Message)*

- Not only did He create us in His nature as leaders, He also commanded us and expects us to lead. He used the words; "Take Charge, Be Responsible." This in essence implies that we have a mandate to lead, nothing less, nothing more. It's neither a choice nor an option; It is a command.

One of the reasons why godly leadership is missing in our society today can be attributed to the fact that our leaders do not take the cue from God as they seek to develop and grow their leadership.

Lee Robertson said that everything rises and falls on leadership. Indeed for any venture to succeed, there must be somebody or a group of persons who are in charge. If there is no one in charge, any institution – be it church, business or government – will not stand. Of course the opposite proves to be true.

If leadership is this important, then we are drawn to ask ourselves this question "What is Leadership? Is it the one and only solution to the problems that we face in this world that we live in?"

The Old Testament is full of examples of leaders. Some succeeded while others failed in their leadership. There is plenty to learn from Moses, Joshua, David, Esther, Joseph and especially Jeremiah; from whose calling the principles shared in this book are derived.

In the New Testament, Jesus is our model leader. Jesus was born to Mary and his adopted father Joseph in the town of Galilee. His birth was unique since his conception was through the Holy Spirit. He was God in human body. Jesus understood his position as a Leader and declared it in the Synagogue in Galilee when he said; *"The spirit of the Lord is upon me, because He has anointed me to preach the good news to the poor . . ."* Luke 4:18-19.

Jesus had a clear sense of focus and purpose for his leadership role. He clearly stated his responsibility in this world as God had directed him to. He not only understood but clearly communicated his leadership role in the redemption of mankind.

1Jesus Christ bought the church with His blood and He is its model leader. For you to learn from the model leader, you need to regard the Bible as the sole authority for faith and practice which is one of the distinctive features of a true church. That is how Christians draw on Jesus' teaching concerning leadership.

Jesus did not only indicate His understanding of his role as a leader; but He also gave us a model, which is the key to success in leadership; Servant Leadership.

Jesus Christ came into the world for the first time to die for our sins. But before he died on the cross, he chose a core group of 12 disciples in whom he invested his time through teaching about the kingdom of God for three years. Thereafter, he allowed Himself to be crucified, die on the cross and after resurrecting on the third day, charged this core group of followers (called the apostles) to go into the entire world and preach the gospel for the remission of sins to those who believe. This was a tall order for poor people who did not even have a high position in society, not to mention the concerted effort to stamp out the new faith by any means. Yet the faith, which Jude 3 says, *"was once delivered unto the saints"* has now, spread almost to every corner of the whole world.

Ask a room full of leaders to explain what they mean by leadership and no two responses will be exactly the same. Leadership is an elusive quality that can be hard to define. A picture cannot portray it. It is not a discipline that relies on the scientific method. Often a story or powerful narrative best captures its essence. Leadership, at its core, is a very human activity, and qualities like honesty, fairness, and credibility are fundamental and recurrent themes regardless of the leadership situation involved.

Definitions of leadership are somewhat elusive. Warren Bennis writes in *On Becoming a Leader* that "leadership is like beauty: it's hard to define, but you know it when you see it"; and that "The ingredients of leadership cannot be taught. They must be earned."

There are as many definitions of leadership as there have been attempts to define the term. It is one of the most observed yet least understood phenomena on earth.

On his part, Peter Northouse defines leadership as *'the process whereby an individual influences a group of individuals to achieve a common goal.'* Northouse's definition brings out several components that are central to the phenomenon of leadership. To be precise, leadership is a process, it involves influence, occurs within the context of a group and it involves the attainment of a goal.

Does the above definition by Northouse apply to all leadership situations whether in politics, society or church? Whereas this may appear to be a universal definition of leadership, there are specific definitions of leadership that may apply to the context of the church.

Dr. J. Robert Clinton defines leadership as "*a dynamic process in which a man or woman with God-given capacity influences a specific group of God's people towards His purposes for the group.*"

From this definition by Dr. Clinton, there are four profound leadership lessons that we can extract.

- Leadership is a dynamic process- You cannot lead every group or individual the same way.
- Leadership involves giftedness-Which is a God-given capacity.
- Leadership has a major role-It is a platform from which leaders influence.
- Leadership has a goal-Which is to make people aware of their sense of God given destiny.

Henry and Richard Blackaby in their book "Spiritual Leadership" define spiritual leadership as *'moving people on to God's agenda.'* While brief, this definition accurately captures the heart of a spiritual leader. The Blackabys outline seven essential marks of spiritual leadership.

- ***The spiritual leader's task is to move people from where they are to where God wants them to be.*** Once spiritual leaders understand God's will, they make every effort to move their followers from following their own agenda to pursuing God's purposes. People who fail to move people to God's agenda have not led. They may have exhorted, cajoled, pleaded, or bullied, but they will not have led until their people have adjusted their lives to God's will. This is influence.

- ***Spiritual leaders use spiritual means.*** Spiritual leaders work within a paradox, for God calls them to do something that, in fact, only God can do. Ultimately, spiritual leaders cannot produce spiritual change in people; only the Holy Spirit can accomplish this. Yet the Spirit often uses people to bring about spiritual growth in others.

- ***Spiritual leaders are accountable to God.*** Spiritual leadership necessitates an acute sense of accountability. Just as a teacher has not taught until students have learned, leaders don't blame their followers when they don't do what they should do. Leaders don't make excuses. They assume their responsibility is to move people to do God's will.

- ***Spiritual leaders focus on people.*** Leadership is fundamentally a people business! It is not merely about budgets or visions or strategies. It is about people. Spiritual leaders never lose sight of this fact. True leaders enjoy people and make them better for having followed.

- ***Spiritual leaders can influence all people, not just God's people.*** God's agenda applies to the marketplace as well as the meeting place. Although spiritual leaders will generally move God's people to achieve God's purposes, God can use them to exert significant godly influence upon unbelievers.

- ***Spiritual leaders work from God's agenda***. The greatest obstacle to effective spiritual leadership is people pursuing their own agendas rather than seeking God's will. God is working throughout the world to achieve his purposes and to advance his kingdom.

- ***Spiritual leaders hear from God***. The role of spiritual leaders is to move people on to God's agenda. How then do leaders know what God's agenda is? Spiritual leaders must cultivate their relationship with God (John 15:5; Jer. 7:13).

I like the Blackaby's definition because it alludes to the fact that leadership has more to do with God revealing the path or direction that He wants you to take. This requires you to listen and obey rather than follow a man's vision (*Appendix A gives a list of the various definitions of leadership that I have been able to find; you can pick out your favourite*).

In a nutshell, most of the definitions edge on leadership being influence in one-way or another. I strongly agree with this. We have not led until we have influenced people and helped them change their status quo. How lovely it is when the influence is in line with God's expectations of us and the framework of His Word!

Jesus did not only indicate His understanding of his role as a leader; He also gave us a model, which is the key to success in leadership; Servant Leadership. If we can understand and fully utilize servant leadership, we will experience the results of our leadership.

The Executive Leadership Development Institute for Chief Academic Officers of the Coalition of Christian Colleges and Universities define servant leadership as *"Intentional stewardship of one's influence to enable and empower other people to identify and achieve the goals of the community in the service of God."*

A servant leader may be defined as a leader whose primary purpose for leading is to serve others by investing in their development and well being for the benefit of accomplishing tasks and goals for the common good.

Jesus told his disciples, *"You know that those who are regarded as rulers of the Gentiles lord it over them, and their high officials exercise authority over them. Not so with you. Instead, whoever wants to become great among you must be your servant and whoever wants to be first must be slave of all. For even the son of man did not come to be served, but to serve, and to give His life as a ransom for many"* (Mark 10:42 – 45).

Jesus demonstrated servant leadership when he washed his disciples' feet. He served not only those who were close to him like John, the beloved disciple, but also Judas, whom he knew was going to betray him.

Jesus clearly had a different lesson to teach on the exercise of leadership which differs from the standards and expectations of the world we live in. He demonstrated that;

- Serving others is the highest calling a person can receive.

- There is need to give in service more than you will ever receive.

Servanthood is always perceived to be weak leadership and in most cases, is not regarded as leadership at all. Servanthood may be excused in the church but seen as an abomination in the corporate world. The truth however, is that to be successful in your leadership, you will need to be a servant leader, no matter where you are called to lead.

The church is supposed to model leadership for the rest of the world. Jesus clearly taught that Christians are to be the salt and the light of the world. Calvin Miller has this to say about servanthood in the church, "The church everywhere has come under a microscope because of her hypocrisy and corruption. She has really been under the scope of media scrutiny because many of her Pastors and Evangelists have lacked leadership and integrity. Thus the number one quality that must mark tomorrow's leaders is servanthood." Miller's statement clearly indicates to us that the right kind of leadership must be based on Jesus' model. If we have true leadership, then institutions will grow to the next level. Without true leadership, we will remain stagnant in one location or will keep going round in circles.

"What is the greatest need in today's church? It is certain that it is not more money, new buildings, bigger buildings, new workable methods, more workers, or any of the other 'things' we throw at the church's problems. The greatest need of the church is leadership... biblical leadership... effective leadership... spiritual leadership. The right type of leadership can solve the church's problems. The right leader can raise the needed money, build the necessary buildings, recruit willing workers, attract eager followers, and discover new methods to get the job done." This assertion from the *Good Book on Leadership* by Borek, Lovett & Towns, is very clear on the need for leadership in the church today. I am convinced beyond any doubt that this statement not only applies to the church but to the market place as well.

There is a distorted view of leadership in our society and church today. Many leaders both in society and church look at leadership in terms of the position it places them in as well as the perks that come along with the position. The current state of the church and society can be understood from the view that leadership is often looked at as an opportunity to lord it over those being led. Leadership is viewed as an opportunity to serve our interests and agendas as well as fulfill our needs. That's why in political leadership and especially in Africa, people will praise a certain leadership regime because of the benefits they derived from it and talk ill of another if they did not seem to have directly benefited from it. In Kenya for instance, people who served in previous governments and probably benefited in one way or another, will defend that government adherently even in cases where it is evident that whatever the government did was wrong.

> *Many leaders both in society and church look at leadership in terms of the position it places them in as well as the perks that come along with the position.*

In addition to understanding what leadership is, it is also important for one to know what is expected of a leader. After acknowledging and appreciating Jesus' model of leadership, which calls on leaders to be servants, it is important to understand that leadership goes beyond service and must deliver results. Ulrich, Zenger & Smallwood state that individuals wanting to be better leaders need a battery of habits, traits, competencies, knowledge, behavior, style, motives, values, and character, which we call collectively, "attributes." But attributes without results are about as valuable as a playbook without playing the game – a mere academic exercise without real-world impact. Results based leadership means achieving outcomes, not just having great character. This however does not underrate the value of character in leadership, which is a subject very important for any leader and has been discussed in another chapter in this book. The only emphasis here is that leadership must bring about results. Jesus clearly illustrated the need for results when he cursed the fig tree for having no fruits. The results of our leadership must be evident for all to see.

Jim Zablonski captures our Lord's leadership success with this statement "with no marketing budget, no distribution network and no paid staff, Jesus built what some would consider the most successful organization in history." The kind of leadership that caused this to happen is what we will be looking at in the following chapters.

An unknown author had this to write about Jesus' leadership and accomplishements.

> *He never wrote a book. He never held an office. He never had a family or owned a house. He didn't go to college. He never visited a big city. He never travelled two hundred miles from the place where he was born. He did none of the things one usually associates with greatness.*

He had no credentials but himself. He was only 33 when the tide of public opinion turned against Him. His friends ran away. He was turned over to His enemies and went through a mockery of a trial. He was nailed to a cross between two thieves. While He was dying, His executioners gambled for His clothing, the only property He had on earth. When He was dead, He was laid in a borrowed grave through the pity of a friend. Nineteen centuries have come and gone and today, He is the central figure of the human race and the leader of mankind's progress. All the armies that ever marched, all the navies that ever sailed, all the parliaments that ever sat, all the kings that ever reigned, put together, have not affected the lives of men on this earth as much as this man – Jesus Christ.

Today, two thousand years after His death, He is still alive, changing lives and bringing new meaning and hope. Only through Him can true happiness, peace with God and eternal life be found.

- Author Unknown-

The world is full of heroes and heroines who only remain so as long as they are alive. Their impact is felt as long as they are alive and in control. Once out of the scene they are forgotten. Will your leadership follow you to the grave or will it continue to be felt long after you are out of the scene?

In her book, *Bad Leadership*, Barbara Kellerman reveals leadership to be a more complex and fluid subject than traditionally thought with leaders, followers, and context all inextricably linked.

Kellerman suggests that bad leadership can either be ineffective or unethical. To distinguish the two, she suggests that ineffective leadership fails to produce the desired change. For reasons that include missing traits, weak skills, strategies badly conceived, and tactics badly employed, ineffective leadership falls short of its intentions. On the other hand, unethical leadership fails to distinguish between right and wrong. Because common codes of decency and good conduct are in some way violated, the leadership process is defiled.

After looking at hundreds of contemporary cases involving bad leaders and bad followers in the private, public, and nonprofit sectors, Kellerman has found that bad leadership can be divided into seven different types:

- **Incompetent** - the leader and at least some followers lack the will or skill (or both) to sustain effective action. With regard to at least one important leadership challenge, they do not create positive change.

- **Rigid** - the leader and at least some followers are stiff and unyielding. Although they may be competent, they are unable or unwilling to adapt to new ideas, new information or changing times.

- **Intemperate** - the leader lacks self-control and is aided and abetted by followers who are unwilling or unable to effectively intervene.

- **Callous** - the leader and at least some followers are uncaring or unkind. Ignored and discounted are the needs, wants, and wishes of most members of the group or organization, especially subordinates.

- **Corrupt** - the leader and at least some followers lie, cheat, or steal. To a degree that exceeds the norm, they put self-interest ahead of the public interest.

- **Insular** - the leader and at least some followers minimize or disregard the health and welfare of those outside the group or organization for which they are directly responsible.

- **Evil** - the leader and at least some followers commit atrocities. They use pain as an instrument of power. The harm can be physical, psychological or both.

The blame, however, does not fall solely on leaders. "Bad followers are as integral to bad leadership as are bad leaders," observes Kellerman. Kellerman examines how followers, such as close aides and advisors, board members, employees, electorates and more distant bystanders contribute to bad leadership.

This really justifies an African saying that any time you point a finger at someone, three fingers are pointing back at you hence declaring you three times as guilty. We are all guilty of the absence of good leadership in the families and institutions that we are part of because we have failed to rise to the occasion and offer alternate leadership if not to challenge the bad leadership that may be in existence.

The Bible is clear that if you know what to do and do not do it, you are sinning.

"... it is a sin to know what you ought to do and then not do it." (James 4:17 – NLT)

Therefore, we should be aware that it is expected of us to exercise godly servant leadership and not bad leadership that lords over others.

PRAYER FOR THE LEADER

Father, we thank you for your calling to leadership. I pray that you will open our eyes to understand leadership from your perspective.

I pray that you will help both the current and prospective leader alike to learn the principles derived from your Word. May the leader make a choice to be a servant leader so that they can make a difference in someone's life now and forever. May the principles shared in this book impact a leader's life and their leadership journey.

Help us learn from the example of Jesus Christ whose theme was service for greatness.

I pray this in Jesus' name.

Amen.

STOP: CHECK POINT

1. What do you understand leadership to be?

2. What are the various misunderstandings of leadership that exist among us?

3. Are you modeling servant or bad leadership?

Part Two

The Principles

3

LEADERSHIP IS A CALLING

Before I shaped you in the womb, I knew all about you. Before you saw the light of day, I had holy plans for you. Jeremiah 1:5 (Message)

The earliest encounters I had of people called by God were testimonies of missionaries serving in different fields such as education, medical and church development, among others. Some had testimonies of how they had big jobs, sold their property and left the comfort of their developed world to go to Africa and serve the Lord. It was puzzling for me to imagine how one would dare leave his family, relatives and friends just to respond to a call.

My father's testimony of God's call in his life was an example of God's call to leadership as well. How he quit heavy drinking, stopped harassing his family and turned to a fine family man and a preacher, cannot be explained in any other way except God's call in his life. He not only became a preacher but also a leader in the community.

Jeff Iorg states that settling the issue of call is foundational to effective Christian leadership. He further states that being "called" is distinctly Christian leadership.

Many people associate the idea of a calling to church or Christian service. Thinking of a calling in regard to professions or careers then becomes an idea that few people harbor in their minds. Briner and Pritchard state that, "As Christians, we must understand that God has a call on our entire lives, including our careers. To see this differently denies both allegiance to God as our creator and an understanding of the unbelievable price Jesus paid for us on the cross. It keeps us from living fully integrated lives in which all things work in synergy for our good and for the building of God's kingdom. When we consider taking positions of leadership, we need to put out our fleece and seek God's affirmation. We may not hear an audible voice from heaven, but we can know that we are acting within God's will for our lives."

Jeff Iorg observes further that ministry leaders serve in response to God's invitation and at his pleasure, not at our initiative. Throughout the Bible and church history, men and women have responded to God's call and led his people. The demands of ministry leadership are simply too great and the consequences too long lasting to assume these roles capriciously or casually. Ministry leadership is a calling we answer, not a career we pursue.

Any successful leadership is a result of responding to a call and invariably depending on God. The Old Testament is full of people who were called of God as leaders of their people. Moses was called to lead the children of Israel from Egypt to the Promised Land. Joshua was called to complete the work that Moses had started when he died before the children of Israel reached Canaan. Prophet Jeremiah was called and ordained by God before he was born, that he may fulfill God's purpose in his life and generation.

Christ was foreordained as Savior before the foundation of the world (1 Peter 1:20). His first coming was a response to this call and is clear from Hebrews 10:7 where He is quoted saying to the Father, Behold I have come, (in the volume *of the book it is written of me,) to do your will, O God. (NKJV).*

Most people do not think that God called them to the professions they find themselves in. Whether you are in marketing, engineering or teaching, whatever your career, the Lord has placed you where you are for a purpose. We are not where we are by accident or mistake. The Lord reminded Jeremiah that he had a very good plan for him even before he was shaped in his mother's womb.

LEADERSHIP IS A CALLING

Whether you are in marketing, engineering or teaching, whatever your career, the Lord has placed you where you are for a purpose. We are not where we are by accident or mistake.

Hans Finzel expresses the fact that few prepare themselves or volunteer for leadership. It is a calling for the appointed. He continues further to say that this seems to be true across the board – in industry, business and government. And it is equally true and more so in ministry vocations.

Rick Warren explains that regardless of one's job or career, we have all been called to a full time Christian service. Growing up, you may have thought that being called by God was an experience only reserved for missionaries, pastors, and others in "full time" church work. But the Bible says that every Christian is called to the service of the Lord.

If leadership is a calling, what does it mean to be called by God and what does it entail? Are there examples of leaders who have set examples for us either in accepting or rejecting God's call in their lives? Has God called some people and not others or is everybody called to a different task. These and many other questions demand an answer for us to understand God's calling in our lives.

Jeff Iorg defines a call as a profound impression from God that establishes parameters for your life and can be altered only by a subsequent superseding impression from God. From this definition there are three key issues that stand out:

1. **A call is a profound impression from God.** This simply means that a call is an inner experience. It is an impression from God and an inner experience with God. He further observes that a call is something you know you have, you are confident it is real and yet it is often difficult to quantify and explain. In the simplest way to explain it, you know you are called because you know it in your heart. A call is thus a subjective experience with God but always set against a biblical backdrop.

2. **A call establishes parameters for your life.** One's calling establishes parameters —giant parenthesis around their life— that directs one's choices and directs the outcome of one's life. A calling means one can say yes to some things and no to others. This can be difficult for other people to understand.

3. **A call can only be changed by another call.** Since a call is a profound impression with lasting results, it means that the call will not be amended or added to very often. A call is an infrequent experience and once called, you remain faithful to the call until you are called again.

The understanding of the call from this perspective has two implications. First God-called people pursue ministry as a calling, not as a ministry career and hence the goal is not a bigger position, higher paycheck or more prestigious situation. With a calling you serve to fulfill your calling. Secondly those who are called persevere through hard times. Men and women called by God do not quit when circumstances become difficult. Jeff Iorg further states that God-called people stay put, firmly planted, until they receive a subsequent superseding call to a new assignment from God.

When we look through the Bible, we find examples of leaders whom God called in different circumstances and in different ways yet all of them were to accomplish specific tasks which He had called them for. Some were called to be prophets, others to be kings, prime ministers (Joseph in Egypt) and missionaries like Paul. For some, the call was dramatic like Saul on his way to Damascus. For others like Samuel, there wasn't much pomp and glamour.

Some examples of people that God called for his purposes in distinctive ways are:

- **Joseph** – God revealed his calling to Joseph through a dream at a very young age. Enthusiastically, he shared his dream with his brothers and parents, but this did not go well with them. The parents and siblings couldn't imagine serving their younger brother. Yet, their activities as a result of their anger only helped fulfill Joseph's leadership destiny. (Genesis 37)

We need to be careful of the timing and to whom we share the dreams that God has placed into our hearts. If we do it to the wrong people or at the wrong time, we may suffer a lot before the dream is actualized.

- **Moses** - God's call to Moses is clearly seen from the moment he escaped death when all the other children of his age were being killed as a result of the King's decree. The Lord was with Moses even as he went to live in Pharaoh's house. God prepared him for leadership while he was there. The burning bush experience in the wilderness as Moses shepherded Jethro's flock was a culmination of God's call in his life. (Exodus 2)

- **David** – He received his call and affirmation while he was still a shepherd boy taking care of his father's flock in the fields. (1 Sam 16:1-13)

- **Esther** – God called Esther, an orphan Jewess reared by her cousin to be the queen so as to deliver the Jews. (Esther 4:14)

- **Mary** – Her call and appointment to be a vessel through whom the Savior of the world would be born was communicated to her when angel Gabriel visited her. (Luke 11:26-38).

Having looked at examples of people that God called, there are lessons we can draw from their experiences as far as calling from God is concerned.

- **The call to leadership is task specific.** There is a crystal clear role. I cannot identify, from my reading of Scripture, any leader in the Bible whom God called with no specific assignment to accomplish.

God has had a very specific role ordained for every person he calls. Joseph's task was to provide a safety net for the Egyptians and the Israelites were saved from the risk of extinction through hunger. It took a long time for Joseph to accomplish the specific task but he finally did. Moses was called to deliver the Israelites from the Egyptians' hands.

In the New Testament, Jesus came to the world to offer His life as a ransom for our sins. That was His specific task. Paul's specific task and calling was to preach the good news to the gentiles, kings and children of Israel. *But the Lord said unto him, Go thy way: for he is a chosen vessel unto me, to bear my name before the Gentiles, and kings, and the children of Israel: For I will show him how great things he must suffer for my name's sake.* (Acts 9:15-16, KJV).

It is therefore evident from Scripture that God has a specific purpose for each person that He created. "You were born by his purpose and for his purpose" According to Rick Warren, discovering God's purpose for your life will put you on the fast lane to success in your leadership. In his book, *Is God Calling You?* Jeff Iorg says that when God calls, he gives new information about how to live and that when he calls he assigns new responsibility in his kingdom.

Have you discovered the specific task that God has called you for?

- **Make No excuses.** Yield to the power of God that is at work within us. All of us have excuses why we cannot take up the leadership challenge. Jeremiah was convinced that he was only a child and could not possibly be a Prophet (Jeremiah 1:6). Moses believed that because he stammered he could not stand before the king and speak.

Discovering God's purpose for your life will put you on the fast lane to success in your leadership.

Each one has an excuse we fall back to when we want to avoid a responsibility. My excuse when I need to avoid taking a certain responsibility is that there are others who can do a better job than myself. I often forget that God is not looking for perfect vessels but rather a willing vessel that He can perfect for His kingdom's service.

What is your excuse for not taking up the leadership challenge?

- **Recognize the Caller's Identity.** There are many times when we get lost in our activities or the worries and troubles of this world that we fail to recognize God's call in our lives. Failure to recognize God's call in our lives may mean that we do not get to respond as God may expect of us. Three times, Samuel mistook God's call to be Eli's and as a result took longer to respond to God. Moses on the other hand failed to realize God's calling and was only moved by his curiosity to find out what was happening at the burning bush.

Have you realized the call of God in your life?

- **Accept the call by obeying the voice of the caller.** One of the greatest challenges facing human kind in any generation is to have people who have leadership ability and yet they insist on being led.

Jonah knew that God wanted him to be on the ship to Nineveh but he got into one that was headed for Tarshish. I believe that the greatest tragedy today for corporate organizations, governments and churches is to find people who have the call to leadership, hiding from exercising their gifting and calling; and then finding others who can't make headways on leadership at the top, calling the shots. There will be no peace for those organizations until the true leaders accept their call to the leadership challenge and move on to take their rightful positions.

Anthony D'Souza speaks of obedience to the call by saying "Leadership is a calling that God places on individuals whom He wants to use, so as to accomplish His purposes here on earth. These individuals are normally people who are open and obedient to God so that He can use them, to fulfill their purposes and destiny in life as they bring Him the glory." Jeff Iorg states that if God is calling you, obedience is the only desired response.

Have you accepted the leadership challenge in your life, work or ministry?

- **Respond and take action on your call.** It's not just sufficient to accept the call that is necessary for us to be successful in our leadership, but taking up the challenge against all odds. David, as young as he was, decided to act on his call and challenged Goliath. Everybody else must have thought David was crazy but he was responding to God's call to stand up against the 'uncircumcised Philistine' in God's name.

There are many times we underestimate our ability, which hinders us from taking up the leadership challenge.

Responding to God's call has never and will never be easy. However, the most fulfilled people I have met are those who have responded to God's call on their lives. You have a choice to make; respond to God's call or ignore it. The big question remains; for how long?

Have you responded to God's call in your life?

- **The call to leadership is not age or stage of life specific.** The call of God comes to us irrespective of our age, social status or education levels. When Jesus called his disciples they were in different professions. Matthew was a tax collector, Luke was a doctor and of course we cannot forget the fishermen. Jesus called each one of them for a specific task and purpose. This clearly explains why we are in different professions. Some in His kingdom are accountants, marketers, politicians and so forth.

Irrespective of your age, stage in life or profession, the Lord has something for you in His kingdom. You are a valuable and useful asset.

The age at which both Jeremiah and Timothy were called into leadership must have been a puzzle to them. However, the Lord knew that he had sufficiently equipped them for the task that was at hand. Irrespective of your age, stage in life or profession, God has something for you in His kingdom. You are a valuable and useful asset.

Have you ever doubted God's call in your life?

- **Own the Call.** Jesus demonstrated the need to own the call when he said; *"My food, . . . 'Is to do the will of He who sent me and to finish His work'" (John 4:34).*

Once you own your call, you will willingly defend it at whatever cost. In normal circumstances, people defend what they own and value. In regard to professional calling; one of the ways to own the call is by adding value to yourself through training. Improving your skills will make you a better person in the area of your calling.

Have you owned God's call in your life? How valuable is it to you?

- **God's call is all about Him.** The calling in our lives is to bring, glory and honor to God. *"For I have come down from heaven not to do my will but to do the will of him who sent me. And this is the will of him who sent me, that I shall not lose any of all that he has given me, but raise them up at the last day. For my Father's will is that everyone who looks to the Son and believes in him shall have eternal life, and I will raise him up at the last day"* (John 6:38-40).

Jesus set us an example by glorifying God with his life. In His prayer he said: *"I have brought you glory on earth by completing the work you gave me to do. And now, Father, glorify me in your presence with the glory I had with you before the world begun" (John 17:4-5).* The calling is not meant to make us great men and women but to glorify God in our service to him at all times.

Have you ever wondered why God placed you where you are?

Since God's call is a subjective experience, there are always many questions that need to be answered. Jeff Iorg, in his book, "Is God Calling Me?" has attempted to answer what I consider to be four key questions regarding God's call to leadership. These questions are:

1. How does God call people?

2. Who does God call?

3. How do you discern God's call

4. What are the effects of God's call in your life?

Lets explore the responses to these questions.

1. How does God call people?

Jeff Iorg identifies three distinct ways in which the Bible uses the word call. He identifies three types of call that one may experience. First is the universal call to Christian service for all believers. The second one is a general call of some believers to ministry leadership and the third one is a specific call to a unique ministry assignment or a particular ministry position.

> ***a. A universal call to Christian service and growth.*** God calls every believer to Christian service which includes not only serving others but personal growth resulting in changed behavior. This call to Christian service can be expressed through any honest vocation. Every believer's work can and should be an avenue for Christian service. The universal call to Christian service is a call to serve God in every setting — including your hobbies, personal activities, and church responsibilities. Every believer is called to Christian service and is expected to consistently live the call in every area of life.

b. *A general call to ministry leadership.* God calls some men and women to leadership roles in his kingdom. They can be vocational or bivocational, full time or part-time; and occupied with preaching, teaching, administrating, or any other ministerial or missional role. The key issue is leadership.

c. *A specific call to a ministry assignment.* After God calls a person to ministry leadership, will later call him or her to a particular ministry assignment. For instance, God may call you to teach, a general call to ministry leadership through educating others, and then call you to a certain school, college or seminary.

Jeff Iorg also identifies three ways that God calls people. The Bible provides a record of people that God called in a variety of ways, often through unusual means and each person had a unique experience. These biblical examples demonstrate three patterns that God calls people. Jeff states that since God's call is a dynamic process, the three categories of calls only help us understand God's call but do not necessarily put God in a box because God's ways cannnot be reduced to a formula. God calls people through:

a. **Sudden or dramatic experiences.** God called Moses to deliver Israel from Egypt by speaking from a burning bush (Exodus 3). He also called Saul (Paul) to ministry leadership through a blinding light on the road to Damascus.

b. **Reasoned decisions or cognitive process or unfolding process of circumstances God allows.** Spiritual discernment reveals God's hand behind the process and his intentional, methodical revelation through this kind of call.

c. **Prompting of others.** Sometimes God sends a messenger, as when Samuel selected David to be the future king of Samuel. (1 Samuel 16).

God also speaks through the church (or the larger Christian community) to reveal his will.

2. Who does God call?

On the question of who God calls, Jeff Iorg states that God calls real people, with real limitations, and confounds all of us by using us to do his work. He calls people who have baggage from their past. He calls those who never expected it. He calls people others would have never chosen. He calls according to his purpose and plan. God calls people with a vision of who they can become and empowers them to do more than they ever imagined. God calls:

a. *Unexpected people.* God calls unexpected, unpolished people to serve him. God calls people for who they can become by his grace, not for who they already are.

b. *Immoral people.* Three women mentioned in Jesus' lineage—Tamar, Rahab, and Bathsheba—had dubious moral reputations and so did David. God calls people who have sexual sin or abuse in the past but once called, God expects you to uphold the high standard of moral purity expected of ministry leaders.

c. *Anonymous people.* Jesus puts people on his team who will fill a role and work behind the scenes. God calls some people who are completely unknown but these people make significant contribution to God's work. When Jesus called the Twelve, he included James son of Alphaeus and Judas, son of James. We may not have much information on their ministry as we have of Peter, James and John.

d. *Inconsistent People.* God calls and uses inconsistent people such as Abraham and David. They did not live to expectations, made mistakes, disappointed God and others. Jeff Iorg states that God calls you for the potential you have not the perfection you demonstrate and your usefulness to God is based on his consistency, not yours.

3. How do you discern God's call?

How do you really know you are called to ministry leadership or to a specific ministry assignment? There may not be any outright answer to this question. However, Jeff Iorg identifies some characteristics of call experiences which can serve as are signposts to help one confirm if God is calling them.

a. ***Inner Peace*** - An inner conviction about your call will give you strength to endure anything from verbal abuse to financial struggles and even including martyrdom (Phil 4:7).

b. ***Confirmation by others*** - God calls through the prompting of others, but he often confirms his call, no matter how it comes, through other people. Several groups of people in this case may be:

- The input of spiritual leaders who know you well are important sources of confirmation of your call.

- Listen to your family. This requires discernment since families may want a different route for you depending on their faith.

- For the married, listen to your spouse. This is because ministry leadership is a team effort. A commitment from both partners is helpful.

c. ***Effectiveness in ministry-*** which has to do with, you having seen God work through you, appropriate to your skill level and opportunity, to effect spiritual results in people's lives.

d. ***Joy in the ministry-*** A passion for ministry could be an indication of God's calling to ministry leadership. Finding joy in the ministry is about finding satisfaction in working with people. Joy comes from watching people saved and grow into mature believers.

e. ***Realistic expectations about the ministry-*** God-called people enter the ministry for the right reason and with reasonable expectations. The desire to be in ministry should be a response to God's call and not to satisfy one's unrealistic expectations about the ministry.

4. What are the effects of God's call?

God's call uniquely impacts your relationship with God and others by changing your perspective and empowerment for ministry. Assurance of his call gives you confidence, helps you persevere through tough times, gives you appropriate authority to lead, and is a source of humility.

   a. ***God gives you confidence.*** When God calls you to ministry leadership or to a specific leadership assignment, you have confidence in your ability and suitability for the job.

   b. ***God's call aids in perseverance.*** God's call is a call to stand firm in tough times and being prepared to make the costly choice to stand up for what is right and walk away when necessary.

   c. ***God's call infuses appropriate authority.*** When God calls a person to ministry leadership, the expectation is that God will work through that person in a unique or special way. God's people expect God-called leaders to lead.

   d. ***God's call leads to humility.*** Your call to ministry does not make you superior to anyone. You received your call to ministry and hence did not achieve it. You have nothing to boast about since your call to ministry leadership came from God, and God has enabled your positive response.

Jesus' model of leadership development

Jesus ministry lasted for three years. He called men such as Peter and John whose credentials are recorded in Acts 4:13. *"When they saw the courage of Peter and John and realized that they were unschooled, ordinary men, they took note that these men had been with Jesus."* Within his short ministry on earth with staff who were unschooled and who disappointed him from time to time, Jesus' model for leadership has lasted for centuries and is still working. What lessons can we learn from Jesus' model of leadership development?

- **God calls and makes you.** When Jesus called Simon and his brother Andrew, he asked them to follow him. He promised that he would make them fishers of men. "*As Jesus was walking beside the Sea of Galilee, he saw two brothers; Simon called Peter and his brother Andrew. They were casting a net into the lake, for they were fishermen. 'Come follow me,' Jesus said, 'and I will make you fishers of men*' (Matthew 4:18-19).

Andrew and Simon were very conversant with catching fish but Jesus promised to make them fishers of men. This is a clear illustration that most often, we will be called to lead in areas that we are not conversant with. God completes the process of the call by making us who he wants us to be. The apostles went through a time and process of making for the three years they were with Jesus. He defended them; he acted on their behalf and was there for them. That was part of the making they had been promised at the time of the calling.

God completes the process of the call by making us who He wants us to be.

The process of being made takes time. For one to be referred to as a professional in any area of life, it takes rigorous training and testing. This process takes time without which one cannot be referred to as a professional.

How much time do you spend time with the master so that he can reveal his calling for you and make you the person he wants you to be?

We can only be the kind of leaders we are called to be if we allow God to make us to be what he want us to be. The lyrics of the song "Sanctuary" implore on us the need to let God make us the kind of leaders he wants us to be. Bill Batstone writes, *Lord, prepare me to be a sanctuary, pure and holy, tried and true . . . With thanksgiving, I'll be a living sanctuary for you.* May the words of this song be the desire for your leadership.

- **God teaches you.** The call to leadership is a call to life long learning. We need to have a teachable spirit since many times, our calling may lead us to areas that we have little or no knowledge of. Jesus told His disciples,

"But the counselor, the Holy Spirit, whom the Father will send in my name, will teach you all things and will remind you of everything I have said to you" (John 14:26).

Albert Einstein is credited to have said that the day you stop learning is the day you stop living. In my simple interpretation of this statement, when you stop living it means you start dying. Not only is this true about life but about leadership as well.

Every day must be an opportunity to learn how to lead better. There is no time in leadership when one has learned all there is to learn and what is left is to practice. Learning is a continuous process. As leaders we must keep asking the great 'Rabbi' (teacher) to keep teaching us every day.

The day you stop learning is the day you stop living.

According to Wayde Goodall, leaders who get stuck in their own worldview stop growing and stop learning. Every leader must be a life long learner. A leader is a reader and the team they work with is critical to the success of the company.

In our professions, we keep improving our skills by attending refresher courses and seminars. Organizations conduct in-house training in an attempt to keep their staff current and up to date. We must learn from the world. As Jesus said in his prayer for His disciples, we are in the world though we are not of the world. *I have given them your word and the world has hated them, for they are not for the world any more than I am of the world. My prayer is not that you take them out of the world but that you protect them from the evil one. They are not of the world, even as I am not of it (John 17:14-16).*

Have you enrolled in God's school of life?

• **God sends you–** In the same manner that Jesus was sent by God, so did he send his disciples, *"As you sent me into the world, I have sent them into the world"* (John 17:18).

LEADERSHIP IS A CALLING

Jesus did not send his disciples to the synagogues and places of worship but he sent them into the world. We equally have been sent into different parts of the world as accountants, administrators, drivers and teachers. Whatever your vocation, you have been sent as Christ's ambassadors. The priority of any ambassador is to represent and defend his government in a foreign country. As foreigners and sojourners in the world, we have a duty to stand for and represent God's kingdom here on earth.

Are you effectively representing God's kingdom in the profession he has sent you?

- **God's calling interrupts your life.** The twelve disciples that followed Jesus were all "interrupted" individually from their different occupations and lifestyles. To interrupt simply means to break the uniformity or continuity of something. In essence, when you are called into leadership, your life is fully transformed and you are never the same again.

Mary the mother of Jesus is an example of a person whose life was interrupted. Her youth was interrupted and she was chosen as the one to give birth to the messiah. Even if she was very young she allowed God to disrupt her life saying *"Be it unto me according to your word"(Luke 1:38, KJV)*

Jonah had a successful ministry among God's people. God interrupted his read life when he was asked to go to Nineveh and preach against it. (Jonah 1:1-2).

> The disciples were in different professions until the time they were called into the work of the ministry. From the tax collector to the fishermen, this calling was an interruption to their daily routines. There is no indication that the disciples were looking to find something else to do before the call. They were all content in what they were doing (Luke 5).

> Saul was an enemy of the gospel and was out to silence the Church through persecution. After his calling, he became one of the most adherent propagators of the very gospel even unto the point of death (Acts 9:1-9).

Moses was a shepherd in the desert when God came asking him to go and save the Israelites from Pharaoh's hand (Exodus 3:1-12).

Samuel was a small boy serving in the temple when God called him to be his prophet and judge over Israel (1 Samuel 3:1-19).

Ezekiel was a captive in a foreign land when he was called to go to the rebellious house of Israel and speak the words of God (Ezekiel 2:1-7).

We all have hopes and dreams of what our lives will be and what we wish to accomplish. We have plans for our families, finances and even futures. Accepting God's call means allowing Him to interrupt the plan you have for your life.

Will you allow God to interrupt the plans you have for your life?
George Barna identifies eight indicators one can use to evaluate their calling to leadership.

1. **Sensing the Call** —You will have a sense of divine selection for the task. You will have an inner conviction that, as amazing as it may seem, God wants you to lead people for him and to him. You will have a real sense of God's confirmation within you of the fact that you are among the few people whom he wants to use to influence followers to live for him.

2. **Undeniable Inclination** -True leaders are naturally inclined to lead. A person may either be drawn to leadership or have a natural enthusiasm and enjoyment for leadership.

3. **Mind of a Leader** – A leader perceives and thinks differently from others by being a person of vision and focused on the future.

4. **Discernible Influence** – A true leader bears the fruit of effective leadership. If God has called you, He will manifest the call by giving you tangible evidence of a special gift to lead.

5. **The company of Leaders** – Most leaders like to hang out with other leaders. As the common saying goes, "Birds of a feather flock together."

6. **External encouragement** – You will receive affirmation from other godly leaders because leaders know their kind. One time, I had a leader I respect very much evaluate my life and work and commended me for being a leader and not a manager. That was very encouraging for me.

7. **Internal Strength** – God's leaders are always people of great courage.

8. **Loving it** – Leaders called by God love not only the end result but also the process which may include incredible mounts of heartache, controversy and animosity.

The realization that leadership is a calling will cause us to change from haphazardly looking for opportunities to lead, to seeking to understand exactly where or what God is calling us into and being obedient to do that which he has called us to.

There is need to realize that leadership is first and foremost, a call. It is God who calls people to leadership, fully aware that He has put in them what it takes to lead.

PRAYER FOR THE LEADER

Father, I thank you for calling each one of us first unto yourself to relate with you. May you strengthen that relationship. May our relationship be a spring board for discovering your call in our life that we may experience the joy of serving where you have called us to.

What a great joy to experience the satisfaction that comes from serving you when we are sure of our call to service in the organization or ministry we are in.

Be glorified in our lives.

We ask this in Jesus name.

Amen.

STOP: CHECK POINT

1. Have you discovered your calling?
2. How faithful are you to the calling that you have received in your life?

4

LEADERSHIP REQUIRES PREPARATION

Then the Lord reached out His hand, touched my mouth and told me; Look, I have filled your mouth with my words ... Jeremiah 1:9 (HSCB)

Have you ever eaten a meal that is not well prepared? It is quite obvious that when you eat a meal that is not well prepared you risk experiencing stomach upsets or even worse - food poisoning. On the same note have you ever sat and imagined the effects of having leaders in organizations or churches who are not prepared for leadership? The effects are likely to be disastrous.

A number of years ago, public universities in Kenya were accused of churning into the job market 'half – baked' graduates. This was simply an issue of employers feeling that the graduates were not well prepared for the tasks expected of them, Thus the call for adequate preparation of graduates before sending them out.

The experiences we have gone through are very crucial in our lives as leaders. They have a significant influence towards achieving what the Lord has for us in our leadership calling and journey. This however, does not suggest that leaders are only made; I believe there are some people who are born with some innate leadership qualities that develop as they grow.

Most of the biblical and world famous leaders were ordinary people that God prepared for extraordinary tasks. Since most leaders are ordinary, preparation becomes necessary so that they are ready to go an extra mile in accomplishing the extraordinary task that God has set for them.

Preparation for leadership is not an event but a process. This process can be lengthy and painful. However, whatever we go through, we need to ascertain that God is preparing us for leadership responsibilities.

Frank Damazio in his book "The Making of a Leader" says that every leader whom God uses in any capacity must first be prepared to function in that capacity. Proper preparation is the only assurance of a leader functioning effectively, but far fewer people are willing to pay the price of being made ready for the task. God prepared every leader in the Bible before they began to do their full work for Him. Some were in preparation more than others. Each was trained differently. God himself has a tailor-made education for each one of his leaders, depending upon the work to which he has called them. The act of preparation is to make ready, to make suitable, to fit, to adapt, to train, to equip or to furnish.

I must caution though that we must not misinterpret the things we go through as a result of our own mistakes or omissions as preparation for leadership.

John Maxwell states, "God prepares leaders in a slow-cooker, not in a microwave oven." More important than the awaited goal is the work God does in us while we wait. Waiting deepens and matures us, levels our perspective, and broadens our understanding. Tests of time determine whether we can endure seasons of seemingly unfruitful preparations, and indicate whether we can recognize and seize the opportunities that come our way."

The Blackabys point out that most of history's famous leaders have been decidedly ordinary. Many of them were neither physically impressive nor academically gifted. They further note that while today media presents leaders in designer clothes, with fashionable hairstyles and flattering makeovers, many of history's most effective leaders were not physically attractive or considered in any way outstanding, when they were young.

Preparation for leadership is not an event but a process. This process can be lengthy and painful. However, whatever we go through, we need to be assured that God is preparing us for leadership responsibilities.

In his book *The Making of a Leader*, Robert Clinton states that, 'God matures leaders over a lifetime' This is to suggest that each day we live, we are growing in our leadership and at no one time can we claim to have made it. Clinton further suggests a six-stage model for leadership development, which can be very helpful in evaluating your leadership development:

Phase One: Sovereign Foundations

Phase Two: Inner Life Growth

Phase Three: Ministry Maturing

Phase Four: Life Maturing

Phase Five: Convergence

Phase Six: Afterglow or Celebration

- **Sovereign foundations** – This has to do with God's activity during the formative years. Parental love, birth order, childhood illness, prosperity or poverty, loss of loved ones, stability versus constant upheaval – factors over which children have no control. The way in which emerging leaders respond to these factors determines much of their leadership potential.

- **Inner Life growth** – This is the stage in which leaders develop their character as well as their spiritual life. During this stage, people experience conversion and with the indwelling presence of the Holy

Spirit, they are no longer subject to the whims of fate and are in a position to be systematically transformed into men and women who think and act like Christ.

- **Ministry maturing** – At this phase, people make their earliest attempts to spiritual leadership. During this stage one may volunteer to lead a church program, or attempt to share their faith with someone. God uses such experiences to teach one what it means to be a spiritual leader.

- **Life maturing** – This is the stage when leaders begin to focus on their strengths to find leadership opportunities. While in previous stages God was working primarily in the leader, at this phase God increasingly works through the leader. God teaches people about life and relationships through significant life experiences. God matures people through normal experiences of failure and success, criticism and praise, loyalty and betrayal, illness and loss. The growth in the leader's life depends on their reactions to the life circumstances through which God brings them. A positive response to the life events ultimately results into a mature level of leadership.

- **Convergence** – During this stage, the leaders experience merger of their life and work experiences into a leadership role that successfully integrates all they have learned with who they have become. This becomes the leader's signature role for which they are best known and in which they enjoy their greatest success.

- **Afterglow or celebration** – Very few leaders get to this phase. This is because it comes after one has led others for a significant period of time. It's a time of coaching the next generation. There is no point to prove as far as leadership is concerned. At this stage, the leader is respected for who they are and what they represent. This phase is comparable to John Maxwell's fifth level of leadership – Personhood.

LEADERSHIP PREPARATION PROCESS

God develops leaders through a process. Our life is school for God to develop us and hence no experience whether good or bad is wasted. The Bible in Romans 8:28 reminds us taht "And we know that in all things God works for the good of those who love him, who have been called according to his purpose."

God can make a leader out of anybody who is willing to go through a period of preparation by Himself. The Scriptures are full of examples of leaders whom God developed through a lengthy process. Some of them include:

- **Abraham** – Abraham did not become the patriarch of a mighty nation due to his greatness. From Scriptures it is clear that Abraham was an ordinary person; a mere mortal who even lied about his wife and consented to go to bed with the house help at the prompting of his wife. By yielding to the preparation of God, Abraham became the patriarch of a great nation and the father of the faithful. He even earned the title "the friend of God."

  Similarly, our leadership will be developed through our failures, successes as well as challenges in life. Remaining focused in challenging circumstances will help us in the growth and development of our leadership.

- **Moses** – When God called Moses to lead the Israelites from their Egyptian bondage; he did not get him straight from Pharaoh's palace to champion the rights of God's children. He had to be prepared by going through the wilderness experience. The higher the task God wants you to accomplish, the greater and challenging the preparation process will be.

  Moses' life in Pharaoh's palace was not in vain. My presumption is that Moses needed to learn the protocol of going before the king and hence the reason why God chose to take him through that route. In addition, the wilderness experience was vital for Moses' future leadership responsibilities. It hardened him in readiness to face Pharaoh and the other obstacles he faced later in his leadership. Some of the obstacles included rebellion from the people he was leading and being let down by his colleague Aaron, who went on to make the golden calf for the Israelites to worship when Moses was up on the mountain.

Our leadership will be developed through our failures, successes as well as challenges in life. Remaining focused in challenging circumstances will help us in the growth and development of our leadership.

We need to realize that we are no exception as far as our leadership is concerned and that the lessons on leadership can come from unexpected quarters; such as our staff and assistants.

Colleagues may let us down. When they do so, we need to realize that, that is an opportunity to learn and grow our leadership. We must never forget that one of the reasons that God allows us to go through the wilderness experience is so that our resolve to follow Him and lead others may be hardened.

There are leaders whom God prepared after their call. Some of them include:

- **Elisha** – When Elisha received his call, he slaughtered his ploughing oxen and made a feast for the people. He was prepared under the oversight of Elijah after his call.

- **Noah** – When God decided to wipe out all mankind from the face of the earth because of their sinfulness, one man, Noah found favour in God's eyes. God asked him to build an ark so that he and his family could be saved from the floods that God was to bring to wipe out mankind. Noah waited for 120 years before the predicted rains finally came. This was such a long time of preparation as he built the ark.

- **Joseph** - When Joseph's brothers sold him into slavery, he must have experienced a lot of pain as his brothers out rightly rejected him. Things didn't brighten up immediately when he got to Egypt either. He was to endure 14 years of imprisonment for a crime he never committed before becoming the prime minister.

- **Job** - He waited perhaps for a life time, 60 – 70 years, for God's justice. His loss of health and wealth would not waive his devotion to God. He stood firm in the winds of the storm.

- **David** – He shepherded his father's flock in the fields and protected them from attacks by wild animals in preparation to be the king of Israel. The same confidence he garnered from his experiences with the wild animals, is what he used to attack and kill Goliath.

- **Joshua** – His preparation took 38 years to enable him take over the leadership of the Israelites from Moses.

Rick Warren reiterates that God formed every creature on this planet with a special area of expertise. Each one has a particular role to play based on the way they were SHAPED by God. Before God created us he decided what role he wanted us to play on earth. Rick explains the acronym SHAPE, as follows:

- **Spiritual gifts** - These are special God-empowered abilities for serving him that are given only to believers. As a way of preparing us for the works of service, God has given each one of us diverse gifts.

- **Heart** – The Bible uses the term heart to describe the bundle of desires, hopes, interests, ambitions, dreams, and affections one has. Your heart represents the source of all your motivations – what you love to do and what you care about most. Another word for heart is passion. There are certain subjects you feel passionate about and others you couldn't care less about. Some experiences turn you on and capture your attention, while others turn you off or bore you to tears. These reveal the nature of your heart.

- **Abilities** – These are the natural endowments or talents you were born with. Your abilities are a strong indication of what God wants you to do with your life.

- **Personality** – We need all kinds of personalities to balance the church. Paul was right when he asked if all the body were an eye how would we hear and how boring that would be. Besides how would we look anyway (can you imagine one big fat eye!). God made introverts and extroverts. He made people who love routine as well as those who love variety, 'thinkers and feelers', lone rangers and those who love working in teams.

- **Experiences** – Most of the life's experiences which were beyond your control have contributed to shape you into who you are today. God allowed them in your life for the purpose of molding you. Six kinds of experiences that might have helped shape you include:

  - Family experiences- What you learnt while growing up in your family.

  - Educational experiences – Your favourite subjects in school.

  - Vocational experiences – Your most effective and enjoyable jobs.

  - Spiritual experiences – Your most meaningful time with God.

  - Ministry experiences - How you have served God in the past.

  - Painful experiences – The problems, hurts, thorns, and trials you have learned from. 'God never wastes a hurt'.

The Blackabys observe that contemporary writing reveals that most scholars believe leaders are both born and made. They further note that in reality most people can exercise leadership in some area of their life, if they are willing to grow personally and develop certain leadership skills. They observe that people's life experiences can dramatically affect the kind of leaders that they become. Such life experiences include:

1. **Home Life:** The influence of a leader's childhood home is a major factor in leadership development. Some great leaders were nurtured in wholesome, supportive environments while others were not. A high percentage of famous leaders had to overcome major hardships during their formative years. The influence of the childhood home in shaping leaders whether good or bad cannot be assumed. A wholesome background can build a strong sense of self esteem and effective people skills that create healthy leaders. While those born in dysfunctional homes may also rise to prominence, their past can often hinder or sabotage their ongoing growth and success as leaders. The Blackabys point out that a significant number of well known Christian leaders grew up in unhappy homes. By God's healing grace, many of these men and women developed into healthy successful leaders.

2. **Failures:** Many people strive to avoid failure while it exerts a powerful force in making leaders and at the same time it appears to be a prerequisite for leadership greatness. As the Blackabys observe, failure is as universal as it is inevitable. The main issue is not failure but the product of failure is what determines leadership development. Failure does not destroy true leaders but develops their character and leadership skills further. A study of the famous leaders will indicate how a high percentage of them suffered dramatic hardships and failures and more so in their early years of life. Possibly this is what may have led Winston Churchill to define success as "….going from failure to failure without loss of enthusiasm."

3. **Crises:** Events beyond a person's control can either crush an aspiring leader or develop the character and resolve within emerging leaders that enables them to reach greater heights in the future. A wise leader will not become discouraged by crises but rather will build

on them knowing that these experiences are likely catalysts for their greatest personal growths.

4. ***Personal struggles:*** Many of history's renowned leaders experienced difficulty in public speaking while others had their hearts broken as young people. Possibly these early disappointments gave the aspiring leaders both a sense of humble reality and a renewed zeal to achieve something significant in their lives.

5. ***Success through hardship:*** A record of history's famous leaders reveals that many of them suffered major failure, crises, and disappointments that these traumas appear to be a prerequisite to leadership success. A conclusion that can easily be made from the biographies of well known leaders is that none of them enjoyed an easy path to greatness. Possibly had they avoided hardship, greatness would also have eluded them. The most important lesson in leadership development lies not in the experiences, whether good or bad, but in people's response to those events.

The Blackabys note that when people face hardship, they become bitter or fearful and they quit trying. Others suffer similar trial but choose instead to redeem their suffering by learning from their misfortune and growing stronger from the experience. The distinguishing characteristic of successful leaders is that they use their experiences as learning tools and gain renewed motivation from their failures. The authors of *Spiritual Leadership* further observe that failure and personal crises will not disqualify you for leadership. However, failure to learn and grow from your mistakes and hardship may prevent you from becoming the leader God intended you to develop into. God can use adversity to build certain qualities such as humility, integrity or faith deep within your character that could be similarly fashioned through lives of comfort and success.

Most of the Biblical and other famous leaders were ordinary people whom God prepared for extra ordinary tasks. Some of Jesus' disciples were ordinary fishermen whom God prepared through the teachings of Jesus for three years.

From Scripture, we see that Saul of Tarsus, who eventually became Apostle Paul, being a Pharisee of the Pharisees had to go through the teaching of the mosaic law. In addition, God determined that he sit under the feet of Philosopher Gamaliel (Acts 22:3) besides being taught the gospel through the revelation of Christ Himself for three years, as we read in Galatians 1:12-18. All the foregoing is what went into making Paul the very effective teacher that he eventually became. Indeed he has written more letters to the church than any other apostle.

We must always remind ourselves that:

- Leadership is for ordinary people and no one can rightly claim to be the wrong material for leadership as long as he or she is willing to yield to God's preparation.

- Your successes and failures during the time of preparation are an integral part of your leadership development.

- Your experiences are part of the process of developing the great leader in you.

In conclusion it is God who prepares His people for Christian leadership. Each believer needs to yield to the preparation irrespective of what it entails.

PRAYER FOR THE LEADER

Father, we know that you have endowed each one of us with various giftings and allowed us to go through various experiences for a purpose. May you help us understand and appreciate our gifts that we may use them for your kingdom's sake.

Help each one of us to focus on our lives and see the good in the painful experiences we may have gone through. Do not allow life's hurts to be a waste but use them for your glory and honour.

Thank you for preparing us in diverse ways for the edification of the body of Christ.

We ask this in Jesus' name.

Amen.

STOP: CHECK POINT

1. What are some of the ways in which the Lord has prepared you for the leadership tasks you have at hand?

2. What has been your response when the preparation is seemingly endless?

5

LEADERSHIP IS CHARACTER

"For behold I have made you this day. . .." (Jeremiah 1:18)

"Possession of godly character, alone, assures true fruit, lasting influence and durable leadership. No amount of "fancy footwork" or "bells and whistles" ever produced a genuine, godly character."

(JACK HAYFORD)

"There is no substitute for character. You can buy brains, but you cannot buy character."

(ROBERT A. COOK)

On August 8, 1972, President Richard Nixon resigned after a move to impeach him following the Watergate scandal.

In the church, we have examples of Jimmy Swaggart and Jim Bakker whose ministries were seriously affected when their character was questioned in the 1980's. In November 2006, Pastor Ted Haggard, the Senior Pastor of New Life Church in Colorado Springs and President of the National Association of Evangelicals in America was permanently removed from the office of Senior Pastor for accusations leveled against him of sexually immoral behaviour. He also resigned from the office of the president of the Evangelicals Association. It is worth noting that in all the examples given above, the issue at hand is not whether the leaders were guilty or not guilty but an instance where one's character was questioned.

Some people are excellent "fakes." Publicly, they may do an abundance of "Christian deeds" and use the right Christian clichés. But privately, their lives are charades. They aren't listening to God. Their lives are mockeries. A story is told of a young man who had just graduated from law school, set up an office, proudly displaying his shingle out front. On his first day at work, as he sat at his desk with his door open, he was wondering how he would get his first client. Then he heard footsteps coming down the long corridor toward his office. Not wanting this potential client to think that he would be the first, the young lawyer quickly picked up the telephone and began to talk loudly to a make-believe caller. "Oh, yes sir!" he exclaimed into the phone. "I'm very experienced in corporate law . . . . Courtroom experience? Why, yes, I've had several cases."

The sounds of footsteps drew closer to his open door.

"I have broad experience in almost every category of legal work," he continued, loud enough for his impending visitor to hear.

Finally, with the steps right at his door, he replied, "Expensive? Oh, no sir, I'm very reasonable. I'm told my rates are among the lowest in town."

The young lawyer then excused himself from his "conversation" and covered the phone in order to respond to the prospective client who was now standing in the doorway. With his most confident voice, he said, "Yes, sir, may I help you?"

"Well, yes you can," the man said with a smirk. "I'm the telephone repairman, and I've come to hook up your phone!

We sometimes fake the Christian life in the same way as the young attorney did. We say we honor God, but we don't obey Him daily. Preoccupied with self and wanting our own way, we ignore God and yet pretend to be spiritual. Instead of having Christ's character reflected by our lives, our Christianity becomes a mere pretence. The importance of character in the life of a leader cannot be over emphasized. As much as performance and results are important, character is paramount. In our society today, people with no character are entertained as far as they meet the organization's expectations and targets. Ignoring the importance of character in a leader's life is only short-lived as can be seen by the number of organizations winding up or individuals being taken to court for money laundering, mismanagement and other ills. For any organization to rise to higher levels, the importance of character has to be emphasized in all spheres.

Character is the part of a person that makes one different from everyone else. It has to do with one's honesty, integrity, one's morals, values, behaviour and credibility.

Tom Marshall clarifies why character is valuable in the life of a leader when he says that, "Leaders always have to work at their character because it is exposed to public scrutiny more than others and will be tested more than others."

> *Character is the part of a person that makes one different from everyone else. It has to do with one's honesty, integrity, one's morals, values, behaviour and credibility.*

The Lord spoke to Jeremiah in Chapter 1:17 and asked him to say what He (the Lord) commanded him to. Jeremiah was required to deal with issues as they were without twisting them to his advantage. This was an illustration and a test of Jeremiah's integrity.

Character is grounded in integrity. Leaders must be honest, credible and completely trustworthy. A person with integrity will not twist facts for their own personal advantage, is willing to stand up for what is right, keeps all promises, and can be counted on to always tell the truth. A person with integrity makes sound decisions, especially when faced with moments of indecisiveness, temptation and conflict. Without integrity, no leader can be successful. In *Leaders Resource Kit,* David Kadalie lists reasons why we all need to work on our character.

- **Our hearts are deceptive.** The Bible reminds us that *"The heart is deceitful above all things and beyond cure. Who can understand it"* (Jeremiah 17: 9). The Psalmist knew this too well and prayed *"Search me, O God, and know my heart; test me and know my anxious thoughts. See if there is any offensive way in me, and lead me in the way everlasting"* (Psalm 139:23, 24).

- **More often than not, we seek leadership for wrong reasons.** (Matthew 20:17-28).

- **The area of character is one that faces the greatest attack.** (Romans 7, Galatians 5:16-24).

- **Character is the foundation to Christian leadership.** (1 Timothy 3:1- 13;Titus 1:6-9).

- **Without character, we will struggle with our talent/gifts.** (Romans 12:3-8).

- **We forget we will have to give an account one day.** The Bible records *"And there is no creature hidden from His sight, but all things are open and laid bare to the eyes of Him with whom we have to do"* (Hebrew 4:13).

- **We naturally neglect character and focus on other development.** *"But have nothing to do with worldly fables fit only for old women. On the other hand, discipline yourself for the purpose of godliness; for bodily discipline is only of little profit, but godliness is profitable for all things, since it holds promise for the present life and {also} for the {life} to come."* (1 Timothy 4:7-8).

David Kadalie further identifies the following marks of true character:

- **A Transformed heart.** The Psalimist Prayed *"Create in me a clean heart, O God, And renew a steadfast spirit within me"* (Psalm 51:10).

- **A life of Integrity.** *"Having confidence in your obedience, I write to you, since I know that you will do even more than what I say"* (Philemon 21).

- **Authenticity.** *"And when I came to you, brethren, I did not come with superiority of speech or of wisdom, proclaiming to you the testimony of God. For I determined to know nothing among you except Jesus Christ, and Him crucified. I was with you in weakness and in fear and in much trembling"* (1 Corinthians 2:1-3).

- **Transparency before God and the followers.**

- **Daily intimacy with God.** Jesus told his disciples *"Abide in Me, and I in you. As the branch cannot bear fruit of itself unless it abides in the vine, so neither {can} you unless you abide in Me. "I am the vine, you are the branches; he who abides in Me and I in him, he bears much fruit, for apart from Me you can do nothing"* (John 15:4-5).

- **Accountability.** *"Let not many {of you} become teachers, my brethren, knowing that as such we will incur a stricter judgment"* (James 3:1).

- **A Good reputation** – (1 Timothy 3:1-7).

- **Commitment.**

Anyone's success in leadership will be greatly influenced by the consistency of his or her character. (*See appendix B for more character qualities*).

There are many situations where leaders are faced with the challenge of compromising their character on a daily basis. Max Depree states that "integrity in all things precedes all else." The open demonstration of integrity is essential; followers must be wholeheartedly convinced of their leader's integrity. For leaders who live a public life, "perceptions become a fact of life."

The word integrity comes from the Latin word *'integritas'* meaning whole or one-ness. The dictionary defines integrity as a firm attachment to moral or artistic principle; honesty and sincerity; uprightness; wholeness; completeness; the condition of being unmarred or uncorrupted, the original perfect condition. Basically, integrity has to do with consistency in our lives whether we are alone or with other people.

If we are to stand out in our leadership, our character and a life of integrity must stand out for all to see.

According to Charles Watson, a person of integrity lives up to high ideals, not because of law force or social pressures, but because that person is genuinely committed to those high ideals. The person with integrity is not one to bend the rules when it is convenient or when temptations are strong — not even "just this once." This is a person who is incorruptible, and you can tell it. Better still, you can depend on it.

There are so many inconsistent leaders in our society whose following is decreasing by the day. If we are to stand out in our leadership, our character and a life of integrity must stand out for all to see. Henry and Richard Blackaby state that Integrity will gain a leader the benefit of doubt from followers who do not see the vision as clearly as the leader does.

In *Leaders on Leadership*, Jack Hayford identifies several arenas of vulnerability that leaders need to guard against if they truly seek a correctable, teachable, heart toward maintaining utmost integrity. These are:

1. **Matters of Accuracy:** Often, we face the temptation to exaggerate numbers, such as church attendance figures. (This is sometimes done in the guise of "our people need encouragement," when in fact the inflated figures are nothing more than an ego boost for the leader himself.)

LEADERSHIP IS CHARACTER

2. **Matters of Privilege:** Those who have hearts of integrity never seek privileges and when they receive them, they never endeavour to unfairly exploit them.

3. **Matters of Power:** The violation of power will inevitably destroy the very real rule intended to the one assigned the authority.

4. **Matters of perceived prestige:** Fame and recognition, at whatever level, render a leader vulnerable to inappropriate vanity, especially when comparisons are made.

5. **Matters of Moral Purity:** A leader who wants to cultivate a heart of integrity must come to terms with his mind as well as his body.

Here are some great quotes from Jack which I would want you to keep in mind:

- The development of leadership character takes more than the practice of external disciplines, for it involves the heart, not just habits.

- Character relates to more than just devotion, for it involves transformation, not simply inspiration.

- Character transcends obedience to rules, for it involves the Holy Spirit speaking to the inner man, offering more than commandments understood by the mind. Such character involves transparency before, and accountability to other people. It is not merely a private quest for purity; it is not solely a man-to-his-God humility.

George Barna identifies the following characteristics (qualities) of the Christ-like character of a leader:

- A servant's heart
- Loyalty
- Teachability
- Optimistic
- Honesty
- Perseverance
- Values driven
- Even tempered

- Trustworthiness
- Joyful
- Courage
- Gentle
- Humility
- Consistent
- Sensitivity
- Spiritual depth
- Forgiving
- Compassionate
- Energetic
- Self-controlled
- Faithful
- Loving
- Wise
- Discerning
- Encouraging
- Passionate
- Fair
- Patient
- Kind
- Reliable

The Scriptures are full of examples of leaders who lived exemplary lives as far as their character was concerned. Some examples include:

- **Joseph:** As a slave boy in Potiphar's house, his master's wife lusted for him. When faced with a moral challenge at his masters' house, Joseph's response was "how can I do this great wickedness, and sin against God?" Joseph's character and integrity could not allow him even to think of sinning against his God.

- **Daniel:** He wouldn't compromise his diet on ritually unclean food, but ate only vegetables. *"But Daniel made up his mind that he would not defile himself with the king's choice food or with the wine which he drank; so he sought {permission} from the commander of the officials that he might not defile himself. Please test your servants for ten days, and let us be given some vegetables to eat and water to drink."* (Daniel 1:8, 12). He also spoke the truth to the authorities regardless of its unpopularity (Daniel 5:17-29).

- **Job:** He would not 'curse God and die' despite the pain and trouble he had been through.

- **Micaiah:** He was bold enough to tell the truth to the king against the word of 400 false prophets.

On the other hand, there are examples of leaders who compromised their character and the end result for them, their leadership and their followers was disastrous.

- **Moses:** He struck the rock instead of asking for water from it as God had instructed him. This cost him the priviledge of getting to the Promised Land.

- **David:** His character flaw made him plot the killing of Uriah so as to cover his adultery. The consequences were heavily borne by his family.

- **Samson:** His love for life and women caused him to compromise his country's security.

- **King Saul:** He disobeyed God and as a result, God rejected him as king.

Leaders have to guard their integrity at all costs since leadership is pegged on the followers' appreciation of the leaders' character above everything else. The essence of character is not only in church leadership but in the political leadership as well. A Kenyan Newspaper (Daily Nation) carried an article titled *"Will Godly Members of Parliament be our saviours in 2007."* Rev. Mamboleo of Redeemed Gospel Church is quoted to have said that, despite his beliefs that 'righteous people would change the political landscape of the country', the electorate should be careful to look at the individual's character. In the same article, David Oginde of Nairobi Pentecostal Church (now Christ Is The Answer Ministries) added that, greater emphasis should be laid on electing people with integrity and not just those with our preferred religious backgrounds and affiliations.

Wayde Goodall writing about character says that the conscience is a fence, a governor, within us that says, "This far and no further." It puts boundaries around us, protects us and others, and will serve us well when it is healthy and it is obeyed. Somewhere embedded in your character is your conscience. To know a person's character is to know the governor which guides their conscience.

It is important for the leaders to run a diagnostic test in their lives and see if there is evidence of character flaws. Leaders can borrow from the example of David in Psalm 139:23-24 where he says: *Search me, O God, and know my heart; Try me, and know my anxieties; And see if there is any wicked way in me, And lead me in the way everlasting.* (NKJV)

PRAYER FOR THE LEADER

Father, we can only lead effectively if our character is in sync with your expectations. We know that pride, lack of moral purity and abuse of power can be great hindrances to the presence of integrity in a leaders' life.

I pray for leaders whose character has been compromised and their leadership is threatened. Give them yet another chance to begin all over again. For those whose character is still strong and intact, give them the protection they need and keep them safe in your arms.

We ask this in Jesus' name.

Amen.

STOP: CHECK POINT

1. What arenas of vulnerability are you exposed to in your leadership?
2. What action can you take to safeguard yourself against attacks in the arena discussed in the question above?

6

SUCCESSFUL LEADERS DEPEND ON GOD

Jesus said several times, "Come, follow me." His was a program of "do what I do," rather than "do what I say." His innate brilliance would have permitted him to put on a dazzling display, but that would have left his followers far behind. He walked and worked with those he was to serve. His was not a long-distance leadership. He was not afraid of close friendships; he was not afraid that proximity to him would disappoint his followers. The leaven of true leadership cannot lift others unless we are with and serve those to be led."

SPENCER W. KIMBALL

A story is told of a man named Jack who was walking along a steep cliff one day when he accidentally got too close to the edge and fell. On the way down, he grabbed a branch, which temporarily stopped his fall. He looked and to his horror saw that the valley fell straight down for more than a thousand feet. He couldn't hang on to the branch forever, and there was no way for him to climb up the steep wall of the cliff. So Jack begun yelling for help, hoping that someone passing by would hear him and lower a rope or something for him to hang onto.

"HELP! HELP! Is anyone up there? HELP!* He yelled for hours, but no one heard him. He was about to give up when he heard a voice, *"Jack, Jack, can you hear me?*

Yes, Yes! I can hear you. I'm down here."

"I can see you Jack. Are you all right?"

"Yes, but . . . Who are you?"

"I am the Lord, Jack. I'm everywhere."

"The Lord? You mean God?"

"That is I."

"God, please help me! I promise if you get me down from here, I'll stop sinning. I'll serve you for the rest of my life."

"Easy on the promises, Jack. Let's get you down from there then we can talk. Now, here's what I want you to do. Listen carefully."

"I'll do anything Lord. Just tell me what to do."

"Okay. Let go of the branch."

"What?"

" I said, let go off the branch. Just trust me. Let go."

There was a long silence. Finally Jack yelled *"HELP! HELP! IS ANYONE UP THERE? HELP!"*

(AUTHOR UNKNOWN).

Have you ever felt like Jack in your leadership? It is one thing to want to depend on God in our leadership and yet another to actually submit ourselves to Him by accepting to do what He asks us to do. Our desire to depend on God ought to be followed by a deliberate effort to follow through the decision. The Psalmist says, *Commit thy way unto the Lord; trust also in Him; and He shall bring it to pass (Psalm 37:5, NKJV).*

There is no better realization for any leader than to know that they cannot make it on their own strength. Jesus told his disciples, "*….I tell you the truth, anyone who believes in me will do the same works I have done and even greater works…*" (John 14:13 NLT). If we can only walk in the light of His Word, there is nothing that He wants us to do for Him that we cannot accomplish. More often than not, we assume that our knowledge, training, experience and connections, will work to make us successful leaders. The closer the leader's relationship with the Lord is, the better the chances of success and vice versa. We read in Zechariah 4:6 that, it does not take power or might to accomplish something for God. It takes His Spirit.

Moses realized the importance of depending solely on God for success in his leadership. He recognized how weak, ineffective and limited he was as a person and asked God not to send them from Mt. Horeb if God's presence was not to go with them (Exodus 33:15). From Moses' experience, we discover that:

1. **Depending on God gives us rest (Exodus 33:14).** Leadership is such a heavy burden. Leaders carry peoples' problems, concerns as well as sharing in their success and joys. All these can weigh heavily on the leader. We have the assurance that the burden should not be on our shoulders and so we can take it to Him who is able to take care of it.

   The lyrics of the hymn 'What a Friend we have in Jesus' clearly indicate that if we are weak and heavy laden, and cumbered with a load of care, our precious Savior is our refuge. There are many times when leaders carry the burdens of their organizations and this not only affects their families but their health and relationships as well. In some circumstances, leaders may be so tired that they need what David Wilkerson calls the 'salvation of their countenance'. This is simply because what is reflected on their faces is nothing but the agony of their current burdens.

   There is no better realization for any leader than to know that they cannot make it on their own strength.

   Leaders need rest. There are moments when leaders get weary because they do not realize that the work they do need not be borne on their own. They must depend fully on God and draw strength from Him.

When Jethro, Moses father-in-law visited him and watched him sit to judge the people of Israel from morning until evening, Jethro said to his son-in-law, ...*The thing that you do is not good. Both you and these people who are with you will surely wear yourselves out... (Exodus 18:17)*

There are so many leaders in our midst who are tired. They have the assumption that if they took some time off from their daily routines to rest, work will not continue or somehow things will not go well. They forget that one day they will die and the business or ministry will still continue without them. I have come across leaders who will not even take a vacation from their business or ministry for fear of the unknown. Leaders can find encouragement in the words of Isaiah 30:15 *"For thus said the Lord GOD, the Holy One of Israel, 'In returning and rest you shall be saved; in quietness and in trust shall be your strength.' " (ESV)*

The lyrics of the song "Still" by Hillsong United point to the fact that we can only find rest in Christ alone when we know His power in quietness and trust.

> *Find rest my soul*
> *In Christ alone*
> *Know His power*
> *In quietness and trust*
>
> *When the oceans rise and thunders roar*
> *I will soar with You above the storm*
> *Father you are King over the flood*
> *I will be still, know You are God*
> © 2003

2. **Depending on God makes us distinct.** We need to stand out from the rest of the leaders who have been or may come after us

in the organization. The manner in which successful leaders handle the people they lead will be different from how other leaders do the same. This is because successful leaders will have realized that they have an opportunity to move people on to God's agenda. Leaders can move people to God's agenda by depending on Him who called them and who is faithful to the very end of age. I believe that it is human to have the desire to be different.

One of the ways that we can depend on God is by hearing from Him all the time. Andrae Crouch in the song *'We need to hear from you'* expresses the need to hear from the Lord.

We need to hear from you
We need a word from you
If we don't hear from you
What will we do?
Wanting you more each day
Show us your perfect way
There is no other way
That we can live
© *1991 GGI Records*

As leaders, we need to depend on the Lord for:

- **Strength** – There are moments when the strength to lead lacks. During those moments, the desire to quit is normally at its peak and there are all the reasons as well as opportunities to do so. Richard and Henry Blackaby have this to say about discouraged leaders. "Countless discouraged leaders would probably quit their jobs today, but they need the income." Such leaders need the strength that comes from God.

Elijah needed God's strength after winning the war on Baal's prophets. He challenged the worship of Baal at Mt. Carmel. Through God's intervention, 450 Baal prophets were killed. People repented and turned to God. Even after witnessing what God had done, Elijah was discouraged and afraid of Jezebel's threats (1 Kings 19). No matter how victorious and successful our leadership has been in the past, we need the Lord's strength at every moment.

For us to depend on the Lord for strength, we need to wait on Him. Isaiah reminds us; *"But those who hope in the Lord will renew their strength. They will sour on wings like eagles; they will run and not grow weary, they will walk and not be faint" (Isaiah 40:31).*

- **Message** – Leaders need to depend on God for the message they deliver to their followers. God asked Jeremiah to say whatever he commanded him to. Most often, it is easier to invite God to bless our agenda rather than seek His agenda and communicate it to the followers. This underlines the importance of the leaders dependence on God through prayer so that they can give ideas and suggestions that glorify God.

- **Decisions** - Leaders are often faced with various decisions to make on a daily basis. According to Peter Drucker, anyone who is not willing to make decisions is not a candidate for leadership. It's often easy to make decisions based on intuition. This is not the character of a leader who depends on God.

Most often, it is easier to invite God to bless our agenda rather than seek His agenda and communicate it to the followers.

- **Provision** – Leaders have needs just like the people they lead. The needs range from financial to social and spiritual needs among others. Leaders not only represent their own needs but also those of the followers and institutions they lead. The Lord has promised to meet our needs according to his riches in glory. However, this is only possible if we are dependent on Him.

- **Victory** – As you will find out in the next chapter, a leader will often be involved in battles (opposition) both within and without the organization. Some of the battles may be caused by virtue of the fact that people do not like you, your ideas and sometimes, they are just jealous of where the Lord has placed you. Each day the leaders' desire must be to win over the battles that may come along his way. The possibility of the answer to the prayer for the victory over battles is fully dependent on the leaders' dependence on God.

At one time in my leadership journey, I found myself involved in some 'leadership battles'. When I did a personal evaluation to find out whether the fights were as a result of something I had done, I discovered that the person who was the engineer of the battles was settling scores due to a misunderstanding she had with my elder brother in a different organization.

- **Relief from stress** -The leadership responsibility is one that is infested with lots of stress. There is significant level of pressure that comes along with leadership responsibilities. Unless we learn to cast all our anxieties to Him who cares for us, we will sooner or later find our leadership on the edge.

Leadership is almost synonymous to stress. Some of the stress may be as a result of scarce resources, unwilling and troublesome followers and even interpersonal conflicts among other reasons.

THE ASSURANCE

Jesus' ministry in the New Testament began with the call of the disciples and ended with a commission to go into the world and preach the gospel message he had given them.

Even after sending the disciples, he promised a new leader, the Holy Spirit, through whom he was going to continue guiding the church. In fact the disciples were not to leave Jerusalem until this new leader came and took charge. To be guided by the Holy Spirit is to be guided by the Lord since the Holy Spirit is the third person in the trinity.

The Holy Spirit is the one who guided Holy men of God to write the Scriptures. 2 Peter 1:21 reminds us that; *For prophecy never had its origin in the will of man, but men spoke from God as they were carried along by the Holy Spirit.* He is also the one who conceived Jesus and guided His earthly ministry. Additionally, He has guided and empowered the church since the day of Pentecost. But the extent of His operation depends on the believer's yieldedness to God through prayer. Simply described, good leadership continually depends on God through prayer.

Jesus' leadership on earth was dependent on God as evidenced by His prayerfulness. Before launching His ministry, He spent 40 days seeking God through prayer and fasting. The night before He chose the 12 disciples was also spent in prayer. One only needs to study the book of Luke to understand how prayerful our Lord was. The apostles were also men of prayer. The reason why the first deacons were chosen in Acts chapter 6 was to enable the apostles to dedicate themselves "continually to prayer, and to the ministry of the Word."

Most definitions of leadership edge on it being influence which I strongly agree. We will not have led until we have influenced people and helped change their status quo and how lovely if it happens to be godly influence!

Jesus understood the importance of depending on God and promised his disciples to be with them always to the end of age. He also clearly spelt it out that any attempt to accomplish anything on our own volition would be in vain for it is not possible. Jesus said *"If a man remains in me and I in him, he will bear much fruit; apart from me, you can do nothing" (John 15:5).*

There are a host of other examples from the Scriptures of people who depended on God and were victorious. When Nehemiah heard the report of Jerusalem's broken wall and its gates burnt with fire (from his brother Hanani), he knew that he could not get help from anyone else but from the Lord. That's why he prayed, wept and fasted.

David knew and often made it clear that his help was in the name of the Lord, the maker of heaven and earth. He had a clear understanding that even if he was to look up unto the hills, there was no other source of help.

The challenge for most leaders is to avoid the tendency to depend on other people. At times, some leaders will form a council of advisors, friends or consultants whom they can turn to for consultations and advice. As much as this is advisable and profitable, especially for accountability purposes, it's not the ultimate solution. The businesses, churches or families we lead will encounter problems at one time or another. It is apparent that Jesus was equally faced with the common daily challenges we face; people and resource management. He however knew who to depend on; it is the reason why he spent countless nights in prayer and communion with His father.

The closer our relationship with God, the easier it is to depend on Him. The distant it is, the less our dependence on God will be.

Micah exhorts us not to depend on our friends: *"Do not trust a neighbor; put no confidence in a friend"* (Micah 7:5a). Our leadership's dependence on God will be evident by our nature of fellowship and relationship with Him. The closer our relationship with God, the easier it is to depend on Him. The distant it is, the less our dependence on God will be.

Jesus final words on the cross before his death were a clear indication of his total dependence on God. Jesus said, *"Father, into your hands I commit my Spirit"* (Luke 23:46). Jesus knew too well that he can depend on God because he is not a man to renege on his word.

The words from the song "Standing on the Promises" written and composed, in 1886, by Russell Carter confirm that a leader's daily dependence upon the promises of God will make him successful no matter what. This is because the promises of God never fail.

The apostles were men who had the same weaknesses as we have. However, by learning to totally depend on God, their ministries were very successful and they did exploits. The same Peter who denied the Lord Jesus Christ became a strong pillar of the apostolic ministry (2 Corinthians 12:9).

The Blackabys identify six reasons why leaders should pray.

1. Prayer is essential since nothing significant happens apart from God. (John 15:5)

2. Prayer brings the Spirit's filling which is a prerequisite for spiritual leaders.

3. Prayer brings God's wisdom (Jeremiah 33:3). He invites us to call him and he will show us things that we have no knowledge of.

4. Prayer accesses God's power. In Matthew 7:7, he has invited you to, "....*ask and it will be given to you, seek and you will find, knock and the door will be opened for you....*"

5. Prayer relieves stress. Since leadership is synonymous to pressure as a result of the heavy load of responsibility they carry, the invitation in 1st Peter 5:7 to cast all cares on him because he cares, is the right thing for any leader to do.

6. Prayer reveals God's agenda as Jesus modeled this truth in Mark 1:30-39.

Your leadership can also be successful if you will learn the art of depending on God.

PRAYER FOR THE LEADER

Father, depending on you is not always the easiest way for us. Like Peter walking on water, we are overwhelmed by the circumstances surrounding us and we begin to sink at the thoughts of the challenges we may be experiencing in our leadership.

Increase our faith that we may learn to depend on you in all we do. May you cause our leadership to be successful to your glory.

We ask this in Jesus' name.

Amen.

STOP: CHECK POINT

1. What are you easily tempted to depend on?
2. Why is it challenging to depend on God?

7

LEADERSHIP REQUIRES COURAGE

"See I have this day set you over the nations and over the kingdoms to root out and pull down, to destroy and to throw down, to build and to plant." (Jeremiah 1:10)

"Leading is a hard task, and opposition is part of the package."

(P.A. Maken)

"Where you need to go, you have probably never been before and the chances are that not too many people have gone there either. The road is sometimes long, scattered with many challenges and worst of all, it seems incredibly lonely. You will need courage. Many great leaders paid the ultimate price due to the fact that they had the courage to challenge – to be free and the desire to take others with them – Martin Luther King, Gandhi, Jesus Christ, John F. Kennedy, the list is endless. Their courage carried them to their graves. Welcome to the world of leadership. (Kairos International)

The earliest experience of courageous leadership I remember, is from my late dad who was a church minister. At one time, he had an interpersonal conflict with a missionary who was responsible for church development in the region where he ministered. Because of their interpersonal conflicts, the missionary came with a padlock one Saturday morning and locked the church gates to prevent the worshipers from accessing the building for the usual Sunday worship service the following day. No sooner had the missionary left than my dad came with a hack saw cut the padlock into pieces and threw them away. None of their actions is commendable though.

The Blackabys note that courage is not the absence of fear. Courage is being frightened and yet doing the right thing anyway. The difference between great leaders and ordinary people is not necessarily that one knew what to do and the other did not. It is often that they both knew what should be done, but only one had the courage to act.

Mark Twain defines courage as the resistance to fear; the mastery of fear – not the absence of fear.

Oswald Sanders believes that the courage of a leader is demonstrated by his willingness to face unpleasant and even devastating facts and conditions with equanimity and then acting with firmness in the light of them, even though it means becoming unpopular. Human inertia and opposition do not deter him. His courage is not a thing of the moment but continues until the task is fully done.

Charles Watson on his part believes courage is the quality that allows a person to encounter difficulties and danger with firmness, to act bravely. It involves doing what ought to be done when no one is looking or when there isn't something forcing one to act in the right way.

Any one who has had a leadership opportunity can agree that leading can be such a daunting task. My evaluation of leadership today both in the corporate world and church as well is that people get into it for the perks and status it can afford them. Most leaders may not have sat down to count the cost of leading. For such a leader, a little pressure is not taken positively but is perceived as opposition to one's leadership.

Wayde Goodall in his book, Why Great Men Fall, suggests that difficulties, challenges and seemingly impossible situations can be your greatest friend. They force you to look deeper, explore possibilities, pray and dream of other ways you might have ignored.

LEADERSHIP REQUIRES COURAGE

Most leaders may not have sat down to count the cost of leading. For such a leader, a little pressure is not taken positively but is perceived as opposition to one's leadership.

There is an African saying that amplifies this thought. The literal translation of the saying from my language is 'the ornaments of leadership are insults and slander.' This statement explains why leaders need courage.

Leadership is not for cowards. A coward is anyone who lacks courage in the face of danger, pain or difficulty. You cannot survive leadership if you cannot stand insults and slander. There is much more than that which comes as part of the leadership package.

More often than not, the leader is not always the most knowledgeable, wise, rich or famous person. What complicates the leadership role further is the fact that we lead human beings who think, reason and, hold certain prejudices. They want to question anything when they can and not necessarily for any reason.

During the call of Joshua (Joshua 1), God commanded him to be strong and courageous. God knew that the task ahead of him was not simple and hence had to prepare Joshua for the leadership journey that was ahead of him. His responsibilities included crossing the Jordan River and eventually getting the people of Israel to the promised land (one thing that his predecessor Moses did not accomplish).

Our leadership is not any different. There are always tasks to be accomplished. Irrespective of where you are leading, whether in church, business or government, the stakeholders are keenly watching to see if there will be returns on their investment. These expectations and how to fulfill them can be such a challenge. In addition, you will always find that there are other people who are interested in your leadership role and will do anything to 'push you out'.

The reality is:

- "All who lead must learn to cope with difficult people. The call to leadership demands we learn that among those we lead, exists a great many people who will be difficult, perhaps impossible to lead. (Calvin Miller)

- "Leadership is fibrous and tough, not easily torn by discouragement. It is very fluid, filtering through the lifestyles of the led.

More often than not, the leader is not always the most knowledgeable, wise, rich or famous person.

History has records of leaders who gave up and quit. Others had their health affected due to the challenges they experienced in leadership. For those of you in leadership already, as well as those who are aspiring to lead, beware that leadership is not an easy task. In legal terms, 'Caveat emptor' is a Latin word which means 'buyer beware.' Borrowing the phrase into leadership, I would wish to put anyone in or willing to get into leadership on notice to beware. The perks and status will come, but there is a cost to pay for them. Jesus' leadership led Him to the cross and so did that of Paul. These serve as examples of the leadership costs.

I would wish to put anyone in or willing to get into leadership on notice to beware. The perks and status will come, but there is a cost to pay for them.

Here are some reasons derived from Jeremiah why leadership requires courage:

- **Leadership is an exercise of authority.** "*I have set you over nations and kingdoms.*" (Jeremiah 1:10) The exercise of authority is not limited to individuals but also to the corporate, church and community members. As you exercise the authority bestowed on you as a leader, you will cross paths with some of those you lead. Cowards may coil under such circumstances, which is not a good thing for a leader to do. The followers expect their leader to take a stand and make decisions on both popular and unpopular issues. There may be need to make decisions to discipline or release employees who are not meeting the expectations or it might be to reward and promote others. Whatever the case, authority must be exercised.

- **Leadership is an exercise of responsibility.** Jeremiah was given some responsibilities over nations and kingdoms with a task to root out and pull down, to build and to plant. This responsibility given to Jeremiah by God was very specific. Exercising the responsibility entrusted to your position may not be the easiest thing since it requires enforcing and implanting both favorable and unfavorable decisions as far as followers are concerned. Pulling down what has existed for a long time is painful and as a leader you will have to be prepared for resistance.

According to Collin Powell, who has headed armies and government agencies and has been the US secretary of state, leadership is not a rank, privilege, title or money. It is a responsibility.

An illustration of a leadership's exercise of responsibility and authority has been witnessed in Kenya, when the government demolished buildings to clear road reserves for the expansion of roads. It was a painful experience for the property owners but one that had to be done as the government exercised its responsibility to provide better infrastructure for its citizens.

Exercising the responsibility entrusted to your position may not be the easiest thing since it requires enforcing and implanting both favorable and unfavorable decisions as far as followers are concerned.

- **Leadership is an exercise of delegation.** Delegation of responsibilities needs to be accompanied by equal authority to perform the tasks. There are great risks in delegation yet the results for delegating can be fabulous. Insecure leaders are very reluctant to delegate. You can only be secure and willing to delegate once you understand that the position you are in is as a result of God's call and preparation in your life. The greatest tragedy in leadership today is to find a leader whose calling and preparation is to lead ten people, in charge of one hundred or so and vice versa. The result is that some leaders are overstretched and hence stressed while others are underutilized.

As you delegate, you need to weigh someone's abilities and giftedness. Otherwise you may be setting people up for failure by giving them responsibilities beyond their ability. Delegating leadership requires courage simply because the person being delegated to may succeed or fail, which may reflect badly on the person delegating.

Lack of openness in a leader's life can result in suspicion and unnecessary accusations.

- **Leadership is a risk.** Leadership has risks that are associated with it. Accepting the call to leadership then means acceptance of the risks that come along. Some of the risks include the loss of one's privileges, freedom and privacy. Your life is open and exposed to your followers and fellow leaders thus making you vulnerable to attacks from many quarters. Lack of openness in a leader's life can result in suspicion and unnecessary accusations.

  Goodall in his book *Why Great Men Fall,* suggests that all great leaders have strong egos. This comes out in our boldness, sense of assurance, willingness to call hard shots, and aggressiveness. In other words, if we are not willing to take risks, make decisions and push the envelope, we aren't really leading.

- **Leadership is equal to pressure and stress.** The Lord prepared Jeremiah by informing him in advance to accept opposition. (Jeremiah 1:19). However, God assured Jeremiah of His presence for the entire time. The truth is whether your leadership is good or bad, there will be people who will fight you. Paul declares, "I have fought the good fight ..." a clear indication that there are battles to be fought and only the courageous will be victorious.

In his book, *Excellence in leadership*, John White shares some insights on the aspect of leadership most of us are hardly prepared for. The following statements are borrowed from White, to help drive the point home that leadership requires courage. He states that;

- **Leadership has enough stress and tensions in the normal course of events.** However, when a leader becomes the target of personal attacks, those stresses are greatly increased. Following Christ may actually involve us in more stress than we expect. The call to follow is a call to advance from stress to stress. At the same time, it is also a call to grow from strength to strength. We are mistaken when we suppose that stress is an evil that must be avoided at all costs. The same stress that kills can also make us stronger and tougher.

- **Success commonly provokes opposition.** The greater the success, the more the opposition. If the success concern's God's kingdom, opposition (whether in the form of human hostility or of unexplained moods of discouragement and fear) will be satanic in origin. Its ferocity will reflect the importance of and nearness to a specific goal. Attacks will focus on godly leaders. Under such circumstances leaders must not lose sight of two things: the source of the opposition (Satan) and the aim of the opposition (to stop the work).

- **The Christian world abounds in slanderous gossip and libelous statements about Christian leaders.** Exposure to leadership is exposure to gossip. Leaders will constantly face the question as to what they must do in the face of slanderous statements.

In the concluding paragraphs of Chapter 7 in White's book, the discussion about the school of courage is quite informative. He states that like Nehemiah, we live in days when we must let our courage be seen by the way we act and speak. It will help us, perhaps, to realize that true courage does not consist in the absence of fear but in doing what God wants even when we are afraid, disturbed and hurt.

White describes an interesting concept of a tough school of courage which many leaders down the ages have taken. He states that in this course, there are practical classes in opposition, loneliness, misunderstanding and tribulation. Some students quit because classes are so rough, not realizing their value. There are no entrance qualifications. Any Christian may apply for training. And the Principal Himself is available for interviews with every prospective student, at any hour of the day. You have only to knock and you will be admitted into His office.

> *The Christian world abounds in slanderous gossip and libelous statements about Christian leaders. Exposure to leadership is exposure to gossip.*

Bill Hybels, the author of *Courageous Leadership* concludes his book with a chapter on developing an enduring spirit: staying on course. Hybels shares the concept of a graduate school of endurance, which is composed of four courses:

FIRST COURSE: MAKE YOUR CALLING SURE AND STAY FOCUSED

According to Hybels, you must master the material in this class. Paul's advice to Timothy in 2 Timothy 4:5, "...*discharge all the duties of your ministry*" requires you to sort out exactly what God has asked you to do in this world. Fulfill your ministry – nothing more, nothing less! Fulfill the exact ministry that God gave you versus the ministry you dreamed up. Not the ministry that forces you out of the basic wiring pattern that God gave you. Fulfill YOUR ministry. The one that flows out of a sincere spirit of humility and submission. The "right" ministry will correspond with your true spiritual gifts, passions, and talents.

Ministry leaders who have lasted the test of time often say that their secret is not attached to anything they "did" – but rather, to the many things that they "did not do." They understand that the key to leadership survival is staying focused.

These leaders have successfully said "No" to anything and everything that would take them or their ministries away from the specific ministry God has given them. They often say: "No, that's not my calling. That's not my assignment. I'm sure heaven has instructed someone to do that, but it's not me." If we invest our limited time, energy, and resources into some of the endeavors we're invited to join, we would have to take away some degree of our time, energy, and resources from what God is asking us to do.

2 Chronicles 16:9 says, *"The eyes of the Lord search all over the world (to do what?) to strongly support those whose hearts are fully His."* This means that if leaders are fully obedient to the calling God has put on their lives, then He will strongly support them in fulfilling that calling.

God knows what He's doing and He's not playing games with our lives. So, when our lives feel unsustainable, we need to turn our attention to what we might be doing wrong. There's always room for improvement.

The words of Paul should haunt/inspire every leader… Fulfill your ministry. Don't bail. Don't quit. Figure out what you need to do to sustain your life in ministry, because quitting is not an option.

In the end, every Christian leader has to get his or her answers from the Holy Spirit. Lay your heart open before the Holy Spirit and say, "God lead my life. You are the Potter, I am the clay. Show me the way. You speak and I'll listen." Every leader must learn Holy Spirit dependence. If you do, God will make your calling sure.

SECOND COURSE: ENDURING BY DEVELOPING THE COURAGE TO CHANGE

According to 1 Timothy 4:16, examine yourself and examine your life. Then change whatever you can change that will lighten your load and help you prevail in your calling. Leaders who have disqualified themselves from ministry often say they didn't have the guts to change and do what was necessary to stay engaged in the ministry. They chose to bail out before they would risk ruffling feathers.

It takes great courage to make the tough decision that increases ministerial sustainability. But we can – and we must – make those decisions.

The point is that sustainability requires intentional solution-side thinking and the courage to stick with a new approach even when you encounter resistance. Often the price seems high, but in the end it is worth it.

Making difficult personal changes: sometimes the change can be awkward, difficult, and painful. The risk of receiving people's disapproval and of damaging your followers can be very real and very frightening but it must be done.

How do you handle the things you can't change… Hybels says, the Apostle Paul had a troublesome condition that he referred to as a "thorn." Apparently it never went away. All of us have a thorn that forces us to turn to God daily and say, "Darn it, God, it hurts again today. For the life of me I don't understand why you don't remove this. But there's a reason why you are God and I am me. I'll trust you through another day. In other words, you talk to God about it, expressing your frustration. But eventually you claim God's words to Paul, *"My grace is sufficient for you"* (2 Corinthians 12:9). Another way to handle thorns is to pray… ask God, "Lord, help me endure this thorn until the sun goes down… we'll handle tomorrow, tomorrow."

THIRD COURSE: ENDURING BY DISCOVERING "SAFE" PEOPLE…

Our hearts were not built to handle the hardships and heartbreaks of ministry alone. We need to link up with a few folks who can help us bear the heavy burdens of our lives. How many more leaders will we lose before we acknowledge our need to lean into "safe relationships?" Galatians 6:2 encourages us to *"Bear one another's burdens and so fulfill the law of Christ."*

Leaders need to find safe people. Keep praying and looking and trusting God to provide such a circle of friends because no one is really strong enough to face the rigors of leadership work alone.

FINAL COURSE: ENDURING WITH AN ETERNAL PERSPECTIVE…

Heroic Christian leaders throughout redemptive history have always looked at the difficulty of their short term struggles against the back drop of eternity. Paul said, in 2 Corinthians 4:17, *"For the light, momentary afflictions that we bear are producing in us an eternal weight of glory far beyond all comparison."* When the difficulties of life appear overwhelming, we need to think more like pilots than sailors. We need to look at the waves from above them rather than in them. That is what it means to look at life from an eternal perspective.

Hybels encourages leaders to "Decide in advance that you are never going to quit. Decide in advance that you are going to keep abounding in the work of the Lord no matter how high the pain level rises. Decide in advance that you are going to keep showing up, trusting, serving, proclaiming the gospel, discipling, shepherding, leading, and casting the vision." That's courageous leadership!

Some examples of Biblical characters who demonstrated the courage needed in the life of a leader include:

- **Esther** – She was ready to go to the King Ahasuerus and argue her case for the Jews, despite the knowledge of the consequences of her decision. (Esther 4:16).

- **Moses** – He needed courage to face pharaoh when God sent him to demand the release of the Israelites from Egypt; notwithstanding the fact that he was a 'wanted man' for having killed an Egyptian. You can imagine the looming danger for a man labeled 'wanted' who must have been hiding for his own safety coming up to the king to petition for human rights abuses. (Exodus 5).

- **Elijah** – He needed courage to challenge the Baal prophets at Mount Camel. (1 Kings 18).

- **Jesus** – He demonstrated courage in many ways. He did not mince words when he confronted the Pharisees and the scribes. He talked about his forthcoming death on the cross even when he knew that it was going to be a painful experience.

- **Jesus' Disciples** – They demonstrated courage during their early days of ministry. When they were commanded not to teach in the name of Jesus in the book of Acts, they choose to obey God rather than men. (Acts 5:29).

Like Paul, we can endure if we have the right perspective. Paul encourages us to endure to the end and to be strong and courageous. *"Be steadfast, immovable, always abounding in the work of the Lord, knowing that your labour is not in vain if it is in the Lord."* (1 Corinthians 15:58). Paul also wrote to the Corinthians and exhaulted them to *"Watch, stand fast in the faith, be brave, be strong."* (1 Corinthians 16:13).

Kalungu-Banda states that great leaders have courage. This does not mean absence of fear but rather learning how to recognise your fears, face the harsh realities of your situation, and nevertheless choosing to follow what you consider the right course of action. At first this is not easy to do. Repeated practice will help you build courage as one of your virtues. He further states that courage in leadership also means choosing to restrain the full use of the power you have been given, which implies trusting the loyalty and ability of people around you. This will enable those under you to grow.

> *Great leaders have courage. This does not mean absence of fear but rather learning how to recognize your fears, face the harsh realities of your situation, and nevertheless choose to follow what you consider the right course of action.*

David Kadalie, in his book, *Leader's Resource Kit,* identifies some common characteristics of courageous people. According to him, people who are courageous:

- act and take the first step
- have overcome their fears
- can shed the old for the new
- are willing to take risks
- are true to themselves and not what others want them to be
- listen to the instincts of their heart
- believe in their cause
- have a fearless determination
- stand firm in spite of opposition
- declare their convictions
- speak truth in every situation

- confront and wrestle with obstacles until they win
- live out their values
- make their dreams come alive
- say 'no' when it is easier to say 'yes'
- tolerate maximum amounts of stress
- take charge of their lives
- have a deep faith in their God

Some of the areas where courage is required in leadership include:

1. **Decision-making.** Leaders face the challenge of decision making from time to time. In the book of Daniel, the Bible records the story of Shadrack, Meshak and Abednego who had to courageously choose between worshipping the true living God and the golden image made by the king. The consequence of disobeying the king was so severe and yet they could not postpone the decision. It took courage for them to say no.

   Daniel also had to make a choice of either denouncing his God or risk being thrown in the lions den. It took courage for Daniel, Shadrack, Meshak and Abednego to make such tough decisions despite the consequences.

2. **Communication.** At a time when he was under pressure, Joshua took his stand and declared to the entire nation that *"as for me and my family we will serve the Lord"* (Joshua 24:15). Courage in communication was evident in his resolve to serve God and how he communicated the same to the Israelites.

   When God instructed Noah to build the ark, Noah needed courage to communicate this message at the risk of looking like a lunatic because what he was alluding to had never been experienced, heard or even happened before.

3. **When there is need to provide direction.** Elijah needed courage to challenge the worship of Baal in Israel. His intention was to provide direction and lead the children of Israel to worship the true God. It took courage for him to stand against the multitude and point them to a different direction. From Elijah's example, we learn that as you strive to provide direction to the people you lead, you may have to stand against the majority when the Lord has convicted you to. The majority are not always on the right path. Being a leader may need you to take an unpopular stand at times. This requires courage.

4. **In the face of opposition.** There are many times when the apostles faced stiff opposition as they preached the gospel. During such times, courage was needed to continue preaching even when the establishment commanded them not to teach in Jesus' name.

   You need courage that will keep you strong in the face of storms. Cowardly behaviour will lead you to withdraw when the challenge becomes fierce. Withdrawal is not a mark of successful leadership, but courage is.

THE COURAGE OF NEHEMIAH

The courage of Nehemiah is demonstrated over and over the book of Nehemiah. As much as Nehemiah's story begins with his confession that he was "very much afraid," he did not yield to his timidity. Nehemiah refused to be timid no matter how fearful and unattractive the course before him was. He faced extremely hard situations; discouragement; was slandered by bitter people who were opposed to anything he sought to do; all his efforts were ridiculed and mocked; he finally faced lies. However difficult the situation he faced was, he did not dodge the issue. He knew that God's Cause demands his best service and so he courageously served in spite of all the difficulties. Nehemiah was immovable and was always pressing on to do God's will. When his enemies could not dissuade him from stopping to do the work, they finally hired someone from within Jerusalem to intimidate him. They told this turncoat to do everything possible to discourage and dishearten Nehemiah so God's Cause would not proceed. The saboteur went to Nehemiah and with feigning sincerity said he had discovered a plot to assassinate Nehemiah. He told Nehemiah that the only safety was hiding in the temple, which was a lie but Nehemiah did not know it. Nehemiah brushed the threat aside and said the courageous words in Nehemiah 6:11 " ...*Should a man like me run away? Or should someone like me go into the temple to save his life? I will not go.*"

This same courage is always expected from those serving God (Josh 1:7; 23:6; 2 Chr 19:11; 32:7; 2 Sa 13:28; 1 Co 15:58; 2 Ti 1:7-9; Rv 21:8a; etc.). Even though we face difficult issues we cannot dodge them. Sometimes courage demands we take unpopular actions (Mt 10:34-39). It takes courage to stand against slander that is spread by bitter enemies of God. Everyone tried to get Nehemiah to quit. Everyone tried to scare Nehemiah. But Nehemiah would not quit! He had made up his mind to serve God!

The courage of Nehemiah led him to be UNCOMPROMISING in his service to God (Nehemiah 6:2-4). Nehemiah refused to compromise with the enemies of God who asked him to stop building the wall and meet with them. Nehemiah refused to compromise with his own people who asked him to be more flexible in his attitude (Nehemiah 6:17-18). He refused to compromise when a letter writing campaign was launched against him in an effort to smear his reputation (Nehemiah 6:19). There is a tremendous lesson here that should bolster our courage – DO NOT be intimidated into compromising God's will no matter the source!

When faced with alluring invitations to compromise, to cease the work for God's Cause, Nehemiah's response was very clear – "*I am doing a great work and I cannot come down. Why should the work stop while I leave it and come down?*" *(6:3).* What heroic courage and conviction! Courage is needed to fulfil God's assignments for our lives.

THE COURAGE OF DANIEL

Daniel is a perfect example of a man who lived according to his strong scriptural convictions. He was willing to stand for them even when doing so could have cost him his life.

When King Nebuchadnezzar conquered the nation of Israel, he took several young people to Babylon to train and indoctrinate them into the Babylonian culture. Daniel was a teen at that time. He remained there throughout the reigns of Nebuchadnezzar, his son Belshazzar, Darius the Mede, and Cyrus the Persian. Although Daniel was a foreigner, he influenced all four kings and became a person of great authority. Because he never backed down from his convictions, the phrase, "the God of Daniel" echoed in the chambers of those pagan kingdoms.

To resist the temptations to compromise our standards, we need to follow Daniel's godly example to see how:

- **He stood up for his convictions when he was a teenager.** Early in life, Daniel made up his mind to live as a Hebrew and keep the Law of Moses. His first test came when he was given food and wine from the king's table. Since this food had been offered to idols, he requested a diet of vegetables and water. After 10 days, the king's official found that Daniel and his friends looked better than the other youths.

- **He was convinced that he should be a godly example to others.** Daniel's determination to live in obedience to the Lord set an example for the other Jewish youths who were living in that heathen society.

- **He knew God would hear and answer his prayers.** That's why Daniel had the boldness to hold firm to his convictions and risk requesting a different diet. Since the Lord is committed to answering the prayers of His children who walk in obedience, we can also have this same conviction.

- **He was committed to being true to the Word of God.** When Nebuchadnezzar had an alarming dream (Dan. 4:19-29), the Lord gave Daniel the horrifying interpretation. At that moment, Daniel had to decide whether he would tell the king the truth or conceal it. Despite the danger, Daniel held to his persuasions and delivered the Lord's message to the king. He had the courage to stand by what was right even though the king could have eliminated him.

- **He had a conviction that he was not going to bow down to any other god.** At one point Daniel's three friends who shared his beliefs were put to the test. When Nebuchadnezzar made an image of himself and commanded all the people to bow down to it, Shadrach, Meshach, and Abednego refused, even though they faced being thrown into a burning furnace. They believed the Lord could deliver them. They were willing to die rather than bow down to any other god.

- **He was fully persuaded that God would protect him no matter what.** Daniel could not be bought off or frightened into compromise because he had nothing to fear as long as his convictions were founded on God's Word.

THE CONSEQUENCES OF DANIEL'S COURAGEOUS STAND

As we look back at Daniel's life, we can see the results of his faithfulness in the following ways:

- **He remained obedient to the Lord.** Daniel won his first battle when he refused to defile himself with the king's food. But that was just the beginning of his lifelong obedience to God.

- **He influenced his companions to do the same.** Shadrach, Meshach, and Abednego followed Daniel's example of obedience and also refused to eat the king's food. They were all blessed by God for their faithfulness to Him.

- **His obedience opened doors of opportunity to counsel and influence kings.** If he'd chosen to blend into the culture, the kings probably wouldn't have noticed him. But because he was a person of character who stood up for his convictions, they heard about the one true God. As believers, we make an impact in others' life by bolding living for Christ without compromising our values.

- **God gave him favor with the kings.** Although Daniel was a foreigner who held firmly to his Hebrew beliefs, he was promoted to the highest places of authority by every king he served. Instead of persecuting him for speaking the truth, they raised him up.

- **God endowed him with one of the most important prophecies in His Word.** Because Daniel had remained a trustworthy and obedient servant in the midst of the Babylonian culture, the Lord entrusted him with amazing prophecies about future events.

God is looking for people like Daniel—followers of Christ who will stand by their godly convictions, even in the face of threat or temptation to compromise for profit. Use your God-given convictions to guide your actions.

PRAYER FOR THE LEADER

Father, there are moments when threats and discouragement distract us from our calling to leadership. The easiest option at that time is to give up and quit.

I do pray for courage and encouragement during those times. When tough decisions have to be taken or in the midst of opposition give courage to the leader that he may stand strong.

We ask this in Jesus' name.

Amen.

STOP: CHECK POINT

1. What leadership challenges have you faced before?

2. Why have you held on?

8

LEADERS EXPERIENCE CONFLICT

Conflict is natural, normal, neutral, and sometimes even delightful. It can turn into painful or disastrous ends, but it doesn't need to. Conflict is neither good nor bad, right nor wrong. Conflict simply is

– DAVID AUGSBURGER

. . Your job is to pull up and tear down, take apart and demolish, and then start over, building and planting.

JEREMIAH 1:10 (THE MESSAGE)

Adrian was appointed the CEO of a corporate organization. He happened to have been the youngest person in the corporation at the time not just in age, but also having worked with the company for the shortest time. As a result of his elevation to the higher office, there was conflict among his staff members. The conflict was between those who supported his leadership and those who did not.

As much as Adrian had a blank cheque from his Board of Directors allowing him to do away with the people he was uncomfortable working with, he decided to work on resolving the conflicts. Today, the organization is quite successful and doing well. Adrian's decision to manage the conflicts bore fruit. What I have found interesting with time is the way in which many people wish to deal with conflict. The ideal world for many people would be one without conflict, where all agree on decisions taken and get along with everyone.

This is the very opposite of the real world that we live in. Conflicts are part and parcel of our daily life. More often than not, leaders find themselves in conflict either with fellow leaders, followers, family or whoever else they interact with.

McShane & Von Glinow define conflict as the process in which one party perceives that its interests are being opposed or negatively affected by another party.

When God gave Jeremiah his job description as a prophet in Jeremiah 1:10, it was apparent that Jeremiah was to participate in actions that were likely to bring him into conflict with his followers.

In Jeremiah's exercise of his God-given task to pull up and tear down, disagreements were bound to arise on why, where, when, how, what, even who. The situation hasn't changed today as far as our leadership is concerned. Conflicts will arise as we exercise our leadership responsibility daily.

Jesus instigated conflict especially in terms of the radical ideas that he taught and acted on – in order to promote positive change in the lives of all people. He did not look for trouble, neither did he shy away from it. His teaching in John 6:25-71, is a classic example where his own disciples grumbled.

The solution for our leadership is not to avoid the conflicts but learn how to manage and resolve them. After all, conflict is in the small print of your job description as a leader.

What is Conflict?

Speed Leas & Paul Kittlaus define conflict as two or more objects trying to occupy the same space. Conflict may also be defined as a struggle or contest between people with opposing needs, ideas, beliefs, values, or goals.

One of the ways to manage conflicts is to identify their sources and address them. By so doing, conflicts will be minimized to a manageable level. Mc Shane & Von Glinow identify the various sources of conflicts in organizations as:

- **Incompatible Goals** – One party's goals perceived to interfere with other's goals.

- **Differentiation** – Different values/beliefs. This explains cross-cultural and generational conflict.

- **Task Interdependence** – Conflict increases with interdependence. There is higher risk when parties interfere with each other.

- **Scarce Resources** – Motivates competition for the available resources.

- **Ambiguous Rules** – Creates uncertainty, threatens goals. Without rules, people rely on politics.

- **Communication Problems** – Increases stereotyping, reduces motivation to communicate and escalates conflict when arrogant.

As a leader, it is your responsibility to address these sources of conflict in your leadership so that you can effectively minimize their potential to bring disunity or harm to your relationships.

Paul instructed the Romans to live with one another in peace, *"If it is possible, as far as it depends on you, live at peace with everyone." (Romans 12:18).*

This Scripture clearly indicates that conflicts are part of us but the power to make peace is within us. The greatest challenge we will have in our leadership is making peace with all men and women.

It is worthwhile to note that not all conflict is negative after all. Healthy conflict is good for the persons affected if they can distinguish between the healthy and unhealthy conflict.

Some of the functions of conflict that I have come across are:

- Conflict can lead to improved conditions and growth.

- Paradoxically, conflict increases involvement and involvement increases conflict.

- Conflict has the potential to promote a sense of cohesion.

- Group conflict can influence creativity and productivity.

The Bible has examples of personal and group conflict:

- Conflict between Euodia and Syntyche. *"I plead with Euodia and I plead with Syntyche to agree with each other in the Lord. Yes, and I ask you, loyal yoke fellow, help these women who have contended at my side in the cause of the Gospel"* (Philippians 4:2-3).

- In Acts 6 conflict arose because the Grecian widows were being overlooked, which prompted improved organization and resulted in the involvement of others in ministering to alleviate this conflicting situation (Acts 6:1-7).

- Conflict between two major missionaries who saw Mark differently resulted in two teams being sent out and may have "saved" Mark for the ministry. Though there was conflict from their point of view, neither Paul nor Barnabas is depicted as being in the wrong. They simply had different priorities and perspectives (Acts 15:36-41).

- Jesus Himself aroused conflict. *"Do not suppose that I have come to bring peace on earth. I did not come to bring peace, but a sword. For I have come to turn a man against his father, a daughter against her mother, a daughter-in-law against her mother-in-law— a man's enemies will be the members of his own household"* (Matthew 10:34).

- Abraham and his nephew Lot disagreed in principle and agreed to part company. (Genesis 13:8-12).

One of the ways to manage conflicts is by following a model provided by Jesus in Matthew 18:15 – 22. The three-step strategy entails:

- Going one on one.

- Bringing in an arbitrator.

LEADERS EXPERIENCE CONFLICT

- Taking the problem to a higher authority.

Other ways of reducing conflict especially for a corporate leader as provided by McShane and Von Glinow are:

- Reduce task interdependence by dividing shared resources, combine tasks and use buffers.
- Increase resources, duplicate resources.
- Clarify rules and procedures, clarify resource distribution and change interdependence.

Ed Rowell provides some biblical preventive steps, which can go a long way towards reducing conflict if incorporated in our daily interaction. These steps are:

1. **Listen more than you talk.** *"He who rebukes a man will in the end gain more favour than he who has a flattering tongue"* (Proverbs 28:23).

2. **Speak the truth in love.** *"Instead, speaking the truth in love, we will in all things grow up into Him who is the head, that is, Christ"* (Ephesians 4:15).

3. **Don't allow anger to rule over your life.** *"In your anger, do not sin. Do not let the sun go down while you are still angry, and do not give the devil the foothold"* (Ephesians 4:26-27).

4. **Admit when you are wrong.** *"The way of the fool seem right to him, but a wise man listens to advice"* (Proverbs 12:15).

It takes a combination of the various strategies shared above to manage conflicts.

Jim Van Yperen conceptualizes conflict as the refining fire for leadership. I found several of his thoughts on conflict very interesting. This is what he says;

- Those who view conflict as sin focus on the emotional pain generated by conflict. Afraid to hurt others, conflict is avoided as though it is a sin. People are extremely reluctant to confront, to disagree, to offend or even rebuke. They are like runners who come across a hurdle and stop, hoping the hurdle will go away, or who go around the hurdle, instead of going over it, disrupting all the other runners in the process. The irony of course, is that this promotes what they are seeking most to avoid. Unresolved conflicts do not go away. It only becomes more divisive, resulting in deeper hurt. A 'leader 'who will not confront is not a leader.

- A biblical understanding of conflict changes our perspective. Dangers turn into opportunity. Leadership becomes the art of discovering truth and obeying Christ.

- The spiritual gift of leadership involves hearing and seeing God's vision, motivating and guiding people to follow the vision, making decisions and resolving conflicts on the basis of God's revealed plan.

- The role of leadership is to see, and to keep in view, the big picture. In conflict, this means seeing the battle from God's perspective. That is, looking beyond what is immediately seen, to understand what comes before and after.

- The first instinct of most leaders is to respond defensively when challenged. In conflict, never confront power with power, rather confront power with truth.

Johnson and Johnson describe the following ways in which individuals deal with conflict. Understanding these ways will help you find out which category you belong:

1. **The Turtle (Withdrawing).** Turtles withdraw into their shells to avoid conflicts. They give up their personal goals and relationships. They stay away from the issues over which the conflict is taking place and from the persons they are in conflict with. Turtles believe

it is hopeless to try to resolve conflicts. They feel helpless. They believe it is easier to withdraw (physically and psychologically) from a conflict than to face it.

2. **The Shark (Forcing).** Sharks try to overpower opponents by forcing them to accept their solution to the conflict. Their goals are highly important to them, and relationships are of minor importance. They seek to achieve their goals at all costs. They are not concerned with the needs of others. They do not care if others like or accept them. Sharks assume that one person winning and one person losing settles the conflict. They want to be the winner. Winning gives sharks a sense of pride and achievement. Losing gives them a sense of weakness, inadequacy, and failure. They try to win by attacking, overpowering, overwhelming, and intimidating others.

3. **The Teddy Bear (Smoothing).** To the teddy bears, the relationship is of great importance while their own goals are of little importance. Teddy bears want to be accepted and liked by others. They think that conflict should be avoided in favour of harmony and that people cannot discuss conflicts without damaging relationships. They are afraid that if the conflict continues, someone will get hurt, and that would ruin the relationship. They give up their goals to preserve the relationship. Teddy bears say, "I'll give up my goals and let you have what you want, in order for you to like me." Teddy bears try to smooth over the conflict out of fear of harming the relationship.

4. **The Fox (Compromising).** Foxes are moderately concerned with their own goals and their relationships with others. Foxes seek a compromise; they give up part of their goals and persuade the other person in a conflict to give up part of his goals. They seek a conflict solution in which both sides gain something – the middle ground between two extreme positions. They are willing to sacrifice part of their goals and relationships in order to find agreement for the common good.

5. **The Owl (Confronting).** Owls highly value their own goals and relationships. They view conflicts as problems to be solved and seek a solution that can help them achieve both their own goals and the goals of the other person. Owls see conflicts as a means of improving relationships by reducing tension between two persons. They try to begin a discussion that identifies the conflict as a problem, by seeking solutions that satisfy both themselves and the other person, owls maintain the relationship. Owls are not satisfied until a solution is found that achieves their own goals and the other person's goals. And they are not satisfied until the tensions and negative feelings have been fully resolved.

We cannot afford to bury our heads in the sand like the proverbial ostrich. Conflicts have the potential to kill our leadership as well as the organizations we lead. The best you can do as a leader is to resolve conflicts sooner rather than later. This is one of the habits for winning at life as identified by Ed Rowell in his book, *Go the Distance*. I believe it is a good habit for winning when it comes to leadership as well.

PRAYER FOR THE LEADER

Father, I realise that conflicts can be challenging moments for those involved and can either build or ruin relationships and even organizations.

I therefore pray for leaders who may be in a conflict now that they may come out of it successfully and victoriously. May it be an opportunity for learning and growth.

We ask this in Jesus' name.

Amen.

STOP: CHECK POINT

1. What kind of conflicts have you experienced in your leadership?
2. How have you tried to resolve conflicts in the past?

9

LEADERSHIP IS COMMUNICATION

.. Stand up and say to them whatever I command you. (Jeremiah 1:17)

To effectively communicate, we must realize that we are all different in the way we perceive the world and use this understanding as a guide to our communication with others.

(ANTHONY ROBBINS)

The single biggest problem in communication is the illusion that it has taken place.

(GEORGE BERNARD SHAW)

The art of communication is the Language of leadership.

(JAMES HUMES)

A blind boy sat on the steps of a building with a hat by his feet. He held up a sign which said: "I am blind, please help." There were only a few coins in the hat.

A man was walking by. He took a few coins from his pocket and dropped them into the hat. He then took the sign, turned it around, and wrote some words. He put the sign back so that everyone who walked by would see the new words.

Soon the hat began to fill up. A lot more people were giving money to the blind boy. That afternoon the man who had changed the sign came to see how things were. The boy recognized his footsteps and asked, "Were you the one who changed my sign this morning? What did you write?"

The man said, "I only wrote the truth. I said what you said but in a different way."

What he had written was: "*Today is a beautiful day and I cannot see it.*"

Many of the challenges that are experienced in organizations are a direct result of either failure to communicate or poor communication. Faulty communication leads to confusion and can cause a good plan to fail.

Peter Drucker, in his foreword to a book on communication (Parkinson & Rowel: 1978) states quite bluntly that poor communication contends that we do not know:

- What to say;
- When to say it;
- How to say it; or
- To whom to say it.

Mercy Randa, in her article titled, *Keep all the communications line open*, suggests that communication is the backbone of modern existence but it is usually misused and its role underestimated.

Communication is the exchange and flow of information and ideas from one person to another. It involves a sender transmitting an idea or message to a receiver. Effective communication occurs only if the receiver understands the exact information or idea that the sender intended to transmit.

Leaders are often faced with the communication challenge. This is simply because the leader not only needs to communicate good news but may at times need to communicate bad news as well. In an organizational context, the leader will communicate promotions, good business deals, births and marriages. The same leader will need to communicate job terminations, death of an employee, business deals gone sour among other sad news.

A study by the Hay Group, a global management consulting firm examined over 75 key components of employee satisfaction and found that:

a. Trust and confidence in top leadership was the single most reliable predictor of employee satisfaction in an organization.

b. Effective communication by leadership in three critical areas was the key to winning organizational trust and confidence:

   i. Helping employees understand the company's overall business strategy.

   ii. Helping employees understand how they contribute to achieving key business objectives.

   iii. Sharing information with employees on both how the company is doing and how an employee's own division is doing – relative to strategic business objectives.

Jeremiah is an example of a good communicator. For 40 years, he served as God's spokesman to Judah declaring God's messages of doom, announcing the new covenant and weeping over the fate of his beloved country.

Most of the prophets had the task of communicating to kings, nations and all peoples. Some of the prophets were misunderstood and as a result they paid dearly for the misunderstanding. At other times, people accepted the message from the prophets as it happened in Nineveh and there was repentance and healing. This is a great lesson for leaders.

There are times when you may communicate to your followers and the message is misunderstood resulting in pain and grief. Other times, your message may be well understood, resulting in great joy. Either way, communication for a leader is not an option but a mandate.

The Bible has evidence of various examples of different leaders who had to communicate either good or bad news.

From the beginning, God set an example for all leaders to follow as far as communication is concerned. He gave clear instructions to Adam and Eve on what they were to eat and what they were not to eat and the kind of authority they had over His creation. God clearly communicated His expectations to Adam and Eve. More often than not, leaders fail the test of communicating their expectations clearly so as to be understood. They expect their followers to do things, which they have not clarified. This normally brings a lot of confusion and conflict.

Interpreted from an organization context, God gave Adam and Eve a job description which was clearly spelt out.

Jesus perfected the art of communication in the New Testament. Most of his ministry's achievements were as a result of good communication. The call of the apostles, the miracles he performed as well as the witnessing to the Samaritan woman at the well, were all cases of good communication whose results were positive. It is certain that communication will bring very positive results in any organization when exercised well.

Moses is a good example of a leader who communicated well with his people. He was the one who met God and brought His message to the people of Israel.

Some of the instances from the Scriptures where the message communicated was not 'favourable' include:

- The Lord sent a message to Eli and his family through Samuel. The message was that God would punish Eli's family for the disobedience

LEADERSHIP IS COMMUNICATION

of his sons. This was not a simple message for the young Samuel to pass on to Eli. (1Samuel 3).

- Elijah's message to King Ahab after he had killed Naboth was that *'dogs will lick his blood at the very place they had licked the blood of Naboth'* (1 Kings 21:19.) This was such a hard message to deliver to the king but it had to be delivered all the same.

- Elijah's message to King Ahaziah that he was not to recover but he was going to die. This again was not a simple message the prophet would have been happy to deliver. (2 Kings 1)

- Prophet Micaiah's message to King Jehosaphat that he would loose by going with King Ahab to fight against Ramoth Gilead, is yet another example of an unfavourable message. (1Kings 22)

An unfavourable message is used in this context to mean that the message received was not the message that may have been expected.

In the previous chapter, the need for courage as a leader was discussed. The ability to communicate requires courage, since you do not know what the outcome of the communication process will be.

Max Depree observed that if you are a leader and you are not sick and tired of communicating, you probably aren't doing a good enough job. One thing that you can never do is to over communicate no matter how often you communicate.

Communication is not just about passing information to another person. It has also to do with listening to the other person as well as getting feedback on what you have said. This is very critical for any leader. More often than not, we are so keen on what we say to others that we do not take time to listen to what they have to say to us in return. We haven't communicated yet until we get a chance to receive feedback.

Effective communication will add value to us if:

- We develop a sense of shared vision and direction.
- It clarifies expectations hence reduce stressors.
- It elicits commitment.
- It brings unity where there is shared sense of direction.

Whether good or bad news, you must learn to effectively communicate if you are to achieve desired results. Communication enhances accountability.

One of the best qualities in any leader is accountability for the resources entrusted to their stewardship, ranging from human to physical and monetary resources. In his book, *Pressing on! Why Leaders Derail and What to do About it*, Benjamin M. Kaufman, gives the following six accountability measures :

1. **Office hours:** Leaders who have specified office hours have built in a certain amount of accountability. In essence, the leader keeps a schedule that others are aware of so that they can reach him or her.

2. **Board and departmental meetings:** Not every leader has consistent board and departmental meetings.

3. **Keeping in touch:** Some leaders purposely isolate themselves and others never know how or when to get in touch with him.

4. **Assessments:** Deliberate assessments are a valuable tool for determining one's own progress.

5. **Goal setting and review:** By writing ones goals at the beginning of each year and reviewing them or have someone else review them at the end of the year, the leader has instituted some accountability.

6. **Accountability groups:** These consists of a small number of leaders who meet periodically to encourage and challenge one another.

LEADERSHIP IS COMMUNICATION

Every leader needs to evaluate his or her communication and find out if they have communicated enough.

The Blackabys observe that spiritual leaders don't merely tell stories for the sake of story-telling. They rehearse what God has done, they relate what God is doing and they share what God has promised to do.

PRAYER FOR THE LEADER

Father, we thank you for setting an example in communication since creation. Many times we fall short on communicating our expectations clearly.

Lord, help us to measure up to your expectation as well as to the expectations of those whom we lead as far as communication is concerned. This is not an easy undertaking but with your help, we can make it.

For those leaders who may have had to communicate challenging messages to their followers, give them the confidence to know that they can still do it again if need be. And for those who are yet to, give them courage should the time come.

We ask this in Jesus' name.

Amen.

STOP: CHECK POINT

1. How do you rate your communication as a leader?

2. Can you identify a situation where lack of communication in your leadership

10

AGE IS JUST BUT A NUMBER

The young have aspirations that never come to pass, the old have reminiscences of what never happened.

(SAKI – SHORT STORY WRITER).

Wisdom does not necessarily come with age. Sometimes age just shows up all by itself.

(TOM WILSON)

"Ah, Lord God! Behold I cannot speak, for I am a youth," but the Lord said to me: "Do not say, I am a youth"

JEREMIAH 1:6. (NKJV)

When Joseph Kabila took over the reigns of power in the Democratic Republic of Congo at the age of 31, there was a lot of scepticism about his ability to transition the country into civilian rule through a democratic election. The scepticism was based more on his age than any other criteria. With time, he has proven his critics wrong by bringing some semblance of order in a country that had been at war for a long time.

When Joseph Kabila took over the reigns of power in the Democratic Republic of Congo at the age of 31, there was a lot of scepticism about his ability to transition the country into civilian rule through a democratic election. The scepticism was based more on his age than any other criteria. With time, he has proven his critics wrong by bringing some semblance of order in a country that had been at war for a long time.

Leadership in the African context was and is to a great extent limited to age even to date. The older one became, the more they were and still are viewed as candidates for leadership. This is very unfortunate because leadership ability is not proportional to ones' age. This does not in any way down-play the importance of the experiences and wisdom that one may acquire with age, which is very crucial to one's leadership effectiveness.

I have borrowed the title for this chapter from Pastor Nick, a friend, who is a strong proponent of age being nothing but a number. Nick became the pastor of a church at the age of twenty-five. For six years, he ministered in a church that grew both numerically and spiritually during this time. With no earlier experience and only equipped with a Bible college diploma, the contribution he made in the ministry of the church was significantly evident.

The Scriptures are full of people who God called to leadership in their youth. The book of Jeremiah is the prophecy of a man divinely called in his youth. Jeremiah's response to the leadership calling was that he could not speak since he was a youth (Jeremiah 1:6).

The Lord's response was quite clear that despite his age, the Lord had chosen him to go where He would send him and speak whatever he would be commanded to. If anything, God had already appointed Jeremiah before he was actually conceived in his mother's womb.

Taking Jeremiah's excuse literally, he was telling God that really there might be other people whom He could use. But God in His sovereignty decided to use Jeremiah; his age notwithstanding.

My own leadership experiences have been a challenge. I have had many open doors where I felt that I wasn't the perfect fit for the challenge at hand. However, whenever I have taken the challenge, albeit hesitantly, the results have always been overwhelming and I have been pleasantly surprised.

The Bible has lots to say about youth. Some examples of young people whom God called into leadership and gave them great leadership responsibility include:

Some of the people whom when they were young include:

- **Joseph** – (Genesis 41:46, 50; 22). Joseph was thirty years old when he entered the service of Pharaoh king of Egypt and became the second in Command over all the land of Egypt. He was made overseer in the house of the Captain of the Guard in Egypt when he was just 17. (*Genesis 37:2; 39:1-4*).

- **David** – (1 Samuel 13:14, 1 Samuel 16:1-13, 2 Samuel 5:4). David was a shepherd boy tending his father's flock when he was anointed to replace King Saul whom God had rejected. He entered into the service of King Saul from tending his father's sheep. He was the youngest in his family. **David** was only a boy when he killed a giant. *(1 Samuel 17:42)*.

- **Jeremiah** – (Jeremiah 1). God called Jeremiah to be a prophet when he was only a youth. God confirmed that He had consecrated Jeremiah and appointed him to be a prophet before he was conceived in his mother's womb.

- **Timothy** – (Acts 16:1-5, 1 Timothy 4:12). Timothy was a young **man** when he first met Paul, probably in his early twenties. Paul trained him for ministry. *"Paul, an apostle of Christ Jesus by command of God our Savior and of Christ Jesus our hope, To Timothy, my true child in the faith: Grace, mercy, and peace from God the Father and Christ Jesus our Lord." (1 Timothy 1:1-2)*.

- **Samuel** – (1 Samuel 3:1, 20). Samuel was dedicated as a baby to serve in the temple. Despite his age, all Israel from Dan to Beersheba knew that Samuel was established as a prophet of the Lord.

- **Daniel** – (Daniel 1:8-16). Daniel joined the service of the Nebuchadnezzar king of Babylon not only as a young man but also as a foreigner.

- **Jehoash** was 7 years old when he became King of Judah. *"Jehoash was seven years old when he began to reign." (2 Kings 11:21).*

- **Josiah** was 8 years old when he became King in Jerusalem. *"Josiah was eight years old when he began to reign, and he reigned thirty-one years in Jerusalem. And he did what was right in the eyes of the LORD, and walked in the ways of David his father; and he did not turn aside to the right hand or to the left." (2 Chronicles 34:1-2).*

- **Ruth** was a young widow when she chose to dwell with her mother-in-law to be a blessing to her. *But Ruth said, "Do not urge me to leave you or to return from following you. For where you go I will go, and where you lodge I will lodge. Your people shall be my people, and your God my God. Where you die I will die, and there will I be buried. May the LORD do so to me and more also if anything but death parts me from you." And when Naomi saw that she was determined to go with her, she said no more. (Ruth 1:16-18).*

- **Mary of Nazareth** was a young virgin when she conceived the Savior, Jesus. *(Luke 1:26-33).*

On the other hand, God also called elderly people and used them in great ways. Some of them include:

- Abraham (Genesis 12:1-4). Abram was seventy-five years old when he set out from Harran.

- Moses (Exodus 3:1-22, 7:7). Moses was eighty years old and Aaron eighty-three when they spoke to Pharaoh and

- Noah (Genesis 7:6). Noah was six hundred years old when the floodwaters came on the earth.

It is apparent that leadership is not for a specific class or age group. However, we must be prepared for challenges that we will face when we take up leadership either at an early or later stage in life. By taking leadership responsibility at an early stage one may be despised, ridiculed and even overlooked, ones authority may be questioned, and discouragement may be bound to occur.

Leadership is not for a specific class or age group.

Apostle Paul's exhortation to Timothy in 1 Timothy 4:12 is, *"let no one despise your youth, [age] but be an example to the believers in word, in conduct, in love, in spirit, in faith, in purity."*

ESTABLISHING YOUR CREDIBILITY WITH ALL GENERATIONS AS A LEADER

Every young leader can learn some helpful leadership principles from the story of Michael detailed below. Even though Michael's story revolves around Church leadership, his experience of how to establish credibility with all generations as a leader is worth the read.

Michael Jordan begun his first pastoral leadership role at 24 years old. The church boards that he served with were full of his parents' generation and the other major demographic group was *their* parents' generation, some of who had helped to found the church some 50 years before. Each of the generations represented in the leadership had a different view of Michael and hence their own way of relating to him. For some, he was like a son, with a promising future and great potential but with plenty of lessons to learn. For others, he was like a favourite grandchild, the one who had made good choices and wound up a happily married pastor instead of whatever "worthless" things other kids were doing.

In the same way each generation viewed Michael, they in equal measure created their own problems when it came to issues of authority.

The major concern for Michael, which should also be a concern for every young leader, was how he could establish his leadership over such a diverse group and how he could avoid being a mascot, prized for cuteness and youth but not taken seriously in the pulpit or the boardroom.

Some of the questions that were critical for Michael at the time and remain critical for any young leader today were;

- How was Michael to avoid being a workhorse, willing to do all the jobs his parents' generation were too busy and his grandparents' generation too tired to do?

- How could he speak authoritatively without feeling like he was representing a whole generation, making every conversation about the difference in their ages?

Michael shared some important lessons he learned about the unique challenges young leaders face in establishing authority. These lessons are adapted to make them valuable for any young leader whether in a church, corporate, community or entrepreneurial leadership role.

1. *Integrity is your greatest asset.* You cannot magically create leadership experience that will convince older generations that you can be savvy at serious business meetings and sensitive in situations that require emotional intelligence. But as a young person, you do have a certain unspoiled sense about you. You may come across as naive at times, true, but you likely also possess a certain energy and idealism that has a deep appeal to followers of all generations. At the very least, older, "wiser" folk will be reluctant to disappoint you; at best, they will see in you a chance to make a fresh start and move beyond previous conflicts or difficulties.

Nothing destroys that positive energy and goodwill quite like a breach of integrity. An ill-timed negative comment to a board member about a fellow staff member, a visit to a questionable website on a organizational computer, a failure to return a phone call or e-mail. These may be rather minor errors on their own, but failures like this confirm older followers' worries that you really are not up to the task, or worse, that you do not respect or like older people. Seasoned leaders can afford a few hits here, but younger leaders cannot, since young leaders must rely on integrity to create momentum and energy.

2. ***Receive other generations with joy.*** Related to this is your ability to gratefully receive the gifts other generations offer you. A mature person realizes that every stage of life has strengths and weaknesses because we are shaped by our life experiences. A young father has a certain slant on the world that he did not before he had kids, and will have a still different slant when he is the father of teenagers and then an empty nester.

With the effects of globalisation, we find ourselves in institutions, where every age group—not to mention every tribe, language, people, and nation is represented with their unique perspectives. It is especially important to remember that, as a young leader, your energy and drive to get things done quickly is not the only gift needed to keep the organisation moving forward. The slow and thoughtful elderly leaders are also essential. In his case, Michael initially distrusted the baby boomers' corporate world experience because it did not have that defiant, us-against-the-world attitude he thought was central to the faith. He also sometimes chafed under the older generation, when he felt they were treating him like a kid. He had to learn that these gifts were offered with the kindest of intentions; once he could see that, he could be genuinely grateful for their gifts offered in humble kindness. In turn, they were willing to be grateful to him for his gifts. Authentic gratitude for another generation's contribution helps them to be grateful for the gifts of your youth, rather than threatened by them.

3. ***Be aware of—and honest about—your weaknesses.*** Our world is shaped to a great extent by the schools we went to and the environments we grew up in. Michael's experience in seminary is a good example of how it shaped his view of church leadership, and his relationship with those he was leading. When Michael went to seminary, they talked a lot about clergy self-care. They learned techniques for advocating for themselves at business meetings, in counselling sessions, and in salary negotiations. They learned the importance of taking a day

off each week, and not caving to parishioners who may want the ministers to perform some ministry task on that day. All of this was important. But for a young minister, it painted a picture of a church, which would inevitably take advantage of its pastor, a church either too cruel or too clueless for its own good.

This way of viewing the relationship between pastor and church has its consequences. Self-righteousness is among the most dangerous. In many small churches, there is already a mutual suspicion between clergy and laity. Laypeople sometimes think that clergy have designs on changing the church in an unwelcome way, and pastors are often angry that laity seems to lack their vision. Self-righteousness inflames this delicate situation when the congregation picks up on the pastor's frustration and feels predictably frustrated with the pastor. Self-righteousness is a common coping mechanism for young leaders, and it is reinforced by many of the educational institutions and denominational structures. True, nothing feels quite so good as venting about your benighted institution when you gather with colleagues for a meeting, but it is ultimately that self-righteousness which inclines people to ignore you and erodes your authority. This scenario is equally replicated in the corporate environments where at times there are suspicions that young leaders are out to challenge the old way of doing things and are always on the look out to change the organisation.

4. *Reserve a piece of yourself that cannot be touched.* Being a leader is an intense, at times overwhelming, commitment. For Michael, it is no exaggeration to say that, after "husband" and "father," "pastor" is the title that has most shaped his identity. The seven years Michael spent at his church marked him indelibly and helped him to mature in a way he could never have grown apart from that role. It is as if being a pastor has given him glasses he can never take off. All of his life experience is filtered through those lenses.

Michael says that despite your busy leadership role, it is essential to reserve pieces of yourself, which are not given to others. If you enjoy baseball, get tickets and go—alone or with your spouse or friends. If you desire more education, find a way to take a class, or develop a reading list that no one in the church knows about. Exercise. Go places whatever it takes to renew you for the task and commitment of the work you do, do it.

This is essential to maintaining authority as a young leader. Likely part of what makes you appealing, as a young leader is your energy, your zest for life. The intensity of the leadership responsibility will crush that if you do not intentionally set aside time to be a human being first. To wilt as a human being is to fail as a leader, because it is to fail as a person.

Sometimes organizations realize their need for young leadership; sometimes they don't. If you are fortunate enough to be a young leader in these times, don't waste it by failing to responsibly use the authority granted to you by God and others. Your youth is a gift from God. If you can treasure and use its strengths, and humbly acknowledge its weaknesses, both you and those you lead can grow in grace.

In addition to the principles young leaders can learn from Michael's leadership role in a church, Mac Lake suggests that when someone, especially a young leader first steps into leadership, they should identify a learning pathway that makes sense and helps them progress in their ability to lead at the next level. Even though the list may vary from one organization or person to another, some of the following competencies are important at each level of leadership pipeline for young leaders. They form part of your unwritten job description as a leader.

LEADING YOURSELF	LEADING OTHERS
• Managing Your Time • Setting Personal Goals • Improving Personal Communication • Managing Your Personal Resources • Dealing with Conflict • Leading with Your Strengths • Submitting to Authority	• Casting Vision • Managing Others' Goals • Recruiting Volunteers • Giving Soul Care • Practicing 360 Communication • Resolving Conflict • Aligning People
LEADING LEADERS	LEADING DEPARTMENTS
• Evaluating • Motivating Others • Managing Budgets • Team Building • Decision Making • Leading Meetings • Applying Situational Leadership	• Persevering in Difficulties • Evaluating Systems • Building Morale • Employee Engagement • Hiring, Firing and Repositioning Talent • Mentoring Leaders • Focusing

LEADING ORGANIZATIONS

- Establishing Organizational Value
- Forecasting the Future
- Managing the Leadership Pipeline
- Taking Risks
- Inspiring Others
- Succession Planning
- Practicing Execution

TEN IMPORTANT LESSONS FOR EMERGING LEADERS

According to Stephen Blandino, young leaders are full of energy, vision, passion, and faith. Identifying emerging leaders is essential to building good teams, and established leaders play an instrumental role in their growth and development. After 20 years of leading, Stephen has a few tips he'd like to share with young leaders. These are things he wishes somebody had shared with him. If you work with young leaders, consider how you can help them grasp these ideas.

1. **Put Character at the Top of Your List** - Most young leaders want to prove themselves. It's a natural reaction because you're trying to get people to take you seriously…, which tends to happen when you have a solid track record. But be careful not to sacrifice your character on the altar of achievement. Ruth Barton once said, **"We set young leaders up for a fall if we encourage them to envision what they can do before they consider the kind of person they should be."** What kind of person do you want to be? Work hard to cultivate character so that what you do doesn't outpace who you are.

2. **Make Listening Your Default Response in Meetings** - As a young leader who wants to be taken seriously, you may feel a temptation to continually voice your opinion. However, it's important to realize that when you give voice to your opinions, credibility hangs in the balance. Remember the words of Jonathan Swift: **"It is better to remain silent and be thought a fool than to open your mouth and remove all doubt."** Ask yourself, "Is what I'm about to say helpful, respectful, and beneficial?" Helpful is "what" you're going to say; respectful is "how" you're going to say it; beneficial is "who" will benefit from it. As Jim Collins says, "What's your questions to answers ratio, and how you can you double it in

the next year?" Learn to ask more questions rather than declaring all of your answers.

3. **Develop the Master Skill** - Authors Jim Kouzes and Barry Posner once wrote, "Learning is the master skill. When you fully engage in learning–when you throw yourself whole-heartedly into experimenting, reflecting, reading, or getting coaching–you are going to experience the thrill of improvement and the taste of success. More is more when it comes to learning." You may have graduated from school, but never graduate from learning. Being a lifelong learner is what empowers your relevance for the rest of your life. Eric Hoffer captured it best when he said, **"In times of change, learners inherit the earth, while the learned find themselves beautifully equipped to deal with a world that no longer exists."** Don't be equipped for irrelevance…keep learning.

4. **Sharpen Your Self-Awareness** - All of us are trying to figure out who we are when we are young. That's a natural part of the growth journey. What's sad is when people get older and still lack the awareness of who God made them to be. Increasing your self-awareness while you are young allows "life purpose decisions" to compound over time. In other words, the more you understand how God wired you, the better decisions you'll make about the direction you choose for your life. Good self-awareness always leads to better decisions about jobs, priorities, and time management. To increase your self-awareness clarify your strengths, discover your passions, and reflect on your dreams.

5. **Seek Out Coaches** - Coaching is possibly the most important strategy to help you grow. Seeking out coaches and mentors will push you light years ahead of where you would be if you travelled alone. As Andy Stanley says, coaching helps you go further, faster. Good coaches take A.I.M. (**Assessment, Insight,** and **Motivation**) at your potential and help you close the gaps between who you are and who you have the potential to become.

6. **Establish Your Boundaries** – Too many young leaders have crashed and burned because they didn't put the appropriate boundaries in their lives to keep them healthy. Research suggests that only one-third of leaders finish well. While you're young, establish boundaries to help you protect your family, your relationship with God, your health, your schedule, and your sexual purity. Boundaries provide banks for the river of your life. Otherwise, your life becomes an out of control flood of dysfunction and destruction.

7. **Learn to Work with People** – Stephen says that in his early leadership years, he burned bridges and hurt people because of his own insecurities. He had to learn to cultivate people skills, develop emotional intelligence, foster trust, and build goodwill with people. Bill Hybels said, *"My definition of 'people skills' includes sensitivity to the thoughts and the feelings of others, and the ability to listen—and I mean really listen—to the ideas of others. I'm looking for people who genuinely care for other people, who view others as more than a means to an end."* Stephen gives an example of a young leader he knew who was so forceful with his opinions that he repelled everybody who worked with him. He couldn't attract volunteers because his personality communicated a "my way or the highway" attitude. Your ability to work with people and successfully manage conflict will determine in great part your effectiveness as a leader.

8. **Own Your Mistakes** – You will make mistakes. This isn't even a question. The question is, how will you respond when you make mistakes? You can make excuses, shift the blame, point your finger, laugh it off, avoid the critics, and pretend they never happened…or you can own the mistakes. When you own your mistakes you exhibit a posture of humility and responsibility. When you don't, you actually deplete your credibility. Either way, you reveal your true character.

9. **Grow Your Pain Threshold** – Leadership is painful, and some of your greatest pains will come from your early years of leadership. Lack of experience, poor judgment, and unrefined skills may lead

to some of your pain. Other pain will be the result of people who betray you, gossip about you, or even lie to you. And other pain will stem from the resistance you feel when you try to initiate new changes or launch a new vision. While your goal isn't to create circumstances that foster pain, you must understand a key insight taught by Dr. Sam Chand: **Leaders only grow to the threshold of their pain.** If you fail to grow your pain threshold, you'll always take the path of least resistance. Good leaders don't seek pain…but they don't avoid it either.

10. **Execute with Excellence** – One of the things I love about young leaders is their ability to dream and innovate. This is one reason every team needs young leaders…they keep the organization from becoming stagnate, complacent, and irrelevant. But the great separator between average young leaders and great young leaders is the ability to execute with excellence. It's one thing to dream up brilliant new ideas, but it's an entirely different thing to turn that brilliance into tangible results. Andy Stanley, Reggie Joiner, and Lane Jones write, "Your ministry is perfectly designed to achieve the results you are currently getting." If you're not getting any results, or your results are marginal at best, you have to learn to move from intentions to actions. Execution and follow-through make the difference. Execute with excellence and you'll build credibility with people.

Despite your age, it is possible to press on and successfully lead God's people, you only need to have courage.

PRAYER FOR THE LEADER

Father, we thank you for your call to lead despite our different ages. Help the leader to understand the challenge ahead of him or her despite their age.

For the leaders whose leadership may have been despised or overlooked as a result of age, give them strength and courage.

I pray for wisdom for those questioned and ridiculed whom you have called to lead, that their followers may experience true leadership despite their leaders' age.

We ask this in Jesus name! Amen.

STOP: CHECK POINT

1. Have you ever been or witnessed someone disqualified from a potential leadership position by virtue of your/their age?

2. What was your reaction to it?

3. What leadership competencies do you need to develop as a young leader?

Part Three

What Next?

11

LEADERSHIP: YOUR RESPONSIBILITY

"The greatest leader is not necessarily the one who does the greatest things. He is the one that gets the people to do the greatest things."

—RONALD REAGAN

"Being responsible sometimes means pissing people off."

—COLIN POWELL, ON LEADERSHIP

Now that you know these things, you will be blessed if you do them.

(JOHN 13:17).

Each one of us has a responsibility to exercise good leadership in the institutions and societies that we may find ourselves in. We cannot afford to just blame others and not take responsibility for what we are partakers of.

One of the ways to express our responsibility is by borrowing the 13 gems of wisdom from the lives of smart people as recorded by Charles E. Watson, in his book, *What Smart People do When Dumb Things Happen at Work:*

1. Maintain the right course by adhering to high standards at all times.
2. Make good decisions because they think clearly and insightfully. They do not make self-serving choices.

3. Strive to achieve excellence not gain popularity.

4. Gain sterling reputation by doing what's honorable.

5. Stand up for those things worth standing up for.

6. Attack difficulties immediately and act positively when adversity strikes.

7. Achieve high levels of performance because they act boldly, doing what they believe to be right.

8. Achieve magnificently because they have a sense of proportion. They put the best ahead of the good, the first rate ahead of the second-rate.

9. Find a great course and serve it unhesitatingly and without calculation, thereby achieving magnificently and deriving lasting satisfaction.

10. Go out of their way to create and maintain trust between themselves and others, and between themselves and their organization.

11. Build and maintain amicable and productive relationships. They bring out the best in everyone with whom they interact and get superior results because of it.

12. Stride ahead because they don't get stripped up by their own egos.

13. Continually improve their performance by learning from their experiences.

I strongly believe that the above gems are a characteristic of both good leaders and followers as well. It will be worthwhile to evaluate your leadership in this light and see how well you measure up.

Are you doing enough or is there room for growth?

Bad leadership will not, cannot, be stopped or slowed unless followers take responsibility for rewarding the good leaders and penalizing the bad ones

LEADERSHIP: YOUR RESPONSIBILITY

The exercise of good leadership is not a preserve of the leaders. The followers have a stake in it as well. Barbara Kellerman gives us tips on how to protect good leadership and avoid bad leadership. She suggests that bad leadership will not, cannot, be stopped or slowed unless followers take responsibility for rewarding the good leaders and penalizing the bad ones. This primarily focuses on the type of leadership exercised as a responsibility for both the leaders and followers alike. I fully agree with that suggestion.

Kellerman further suggests the following actions for leaders to strengthen their personal capacity to be effective and ethical:

- **Limit your tenure** – Leaders who remain in positions of power for too long acquire bad habits.

- **Share power** – When power is centralized, it is likely to be misused or abused and that puts a premium on delegation and collaboration.

- **Don't believe your own hype.**

- **Get real. Stay real** – Virtually every bad leader is out of touch with reality.

- **Compensate for your weakness** – leaders need to surround themselves with experts in their areas.

- **Stay balanced** – There is need for the leader to balance their personal and professional life.

- **Remember the mission** – Stay focused on why you exist.

- **Stay healthy** – seek professional help.

- **Develop a personal support system.** – All of us should have aides, associates, friends, or family members who will save us from ourselves.

- **Be creative** – The past should never determine the future nor narrow the available options.

- **Know and control your appetites** – These include the hunger for power, money, success and sex.

- **Be reflective** – Virtually every one of the great writers on leadership emphasizes the importance of self knowledge, self control and good habits.

For the followers, Kellerman suggests the following to resist leaders who are ineffective or unethical.

- Empower yourselves.

- Be loyal to the whole and not to any single individuals.

- Be skeptical – leaders are not gods. They need to earn their loyalty.

- Take a stand – Pliant boards, scared and submissive subordinates are as much to blame for bad leadership as the bad leaders.

- Pay attention – More followers contribute to bad leadership by inattention, either deliberate or inadvertent, than by any other single lapse.

Followers can also work with each other and with their leaders, to get the best work done in the best way possible by:

1. **Ensuring that the punishment fits the crime.** Bad leaders must be made to pay for their transgression.

2. **Find allies** – There is strength in numbers. Powerless people can become powerful by finding other like-minded people to work with.

3. **Develop your own sources of information** – People in authority will not always provide you with correct and complete information.

4. **Take collective action** on a modest scale such as getting a small group together to talk to the boss.

5. **Be a watchdog** – Do not abdicate your responsibility to exercise oversight especially for board members.

6. **Hold leaders to account** by securing transparency, open discussion and meaningful participation.

One basic truth that we cannot run away from is the fact that we have a responsibility whether we are leaders or followers. *Will you exercise it?*

My encouragement to you is that you need to exercise your responsibility no matter what. An unknown writer made the following observations in an article entitled *"Paradoxical Commandments of Leadership"*

People are illogical, unreasonable and self-centred. Love them anyway.

If you do good, people will accuse you of selfish ulterior motives. Do good anyway.

If you are successful, you win false friends and true enemies. Succeed anyway.

The good you do today will be forgotten tomorrow. Do good anyway.

Honesty and frankness make you vulnerable. Be honest and frank anyway.

The biggest men with the biggest ideas can be shot down by the smallest men with the smallest minds. Think big anyway.

People favour underdogs but follow only top dogs. Fight for a few underdogs anyway.

What you spend years building may be destroyed overnight. Build anyway.

People really need help but may attack you if you do help them. Help them anyway. Give the best you have and you may still get kicked in the teeth. Give the world the best you have anyway.

PRAYER FOR THE LEADER

Father, we thank you for the revelation that we have responsibility in the exercise of leadership wherever you have placed us. I pray that you will give each one of us the courage and strength to exercise the responsibility before us knowing that you will hold us to account for our every action.

No matter what we go through, help us to remain focused.

We ask this in Jesus' name.

Amen.

12

FULFILL YOUR LEADERSHIP

I believe that each one of us desires to fulfill our destiny by being the leader that God intended us to be since creation. For you to fulfill your leadership calling there are three basic tenets, which in my opinion, are critical. If you adhere to them, you will most likely succeed. But if you ignore any of them, you can jeopardise your leadership potential. I refer to these tenets as the three C's of fulfilling your leadership calling. These tenets are Commitment, Consistency and Credibility.

Let's look at each of them individually.

COMMITMENT

Leadership has its lows and highs. It is only commitment that will see you through your leadership both in the good, challenging and tough times.

Jesus was committed to his twelve disciples even after they had let him down- which they did over and over again – but he never gave up on them. Again, Jesus was so committed to the salvation of mankind such that even in the face of death on the cross, his commitment did not wane at any given time. If anything, the more challenging things became for our Lord Jesus, the more He was willing to go the extra mile. This was a result of His commitment to the purpose for which he came to earth.

> *Leadership has its lows and highs. It is only commitment that will see you through your leadership both in the good, challenging and tough times.*

For your leadership to be successful, you need to be committed to:

- **Your organization or ministry:** This will be clearly evident by how you spend the resources that God has entrusted to you both physical, financial and human resources.

- **The task entrusted to you:** You have a job to do and how you do it matters a lot. Follow through the tasks entrusted to you.

- **Your followers:** The people you are leading are always looking up to you to see how well you lead them. Your commitment to your followers and their service will set an example for them to follow.

CONSISTENCY

This has to do with keeping to the same principles or course of action at all times. This is a great challenge to many leaders who relate to followers in the organizations they lead at different levels. Some of them have a closer relationship with the leader while others are just but colleagues with no special attachment to them. When faced with a decision to make regarding different people, most leaders' decisions may vary depending on the relationship shared.

> *For your leadership to stand the test of time, you need to be consistent in that it doesn't really matter who the decision will affect but that you stand by the same principles for all people and at all times.*

Jesus, our model leader was consistent in his prayer life and teaching. Daniel was equally consistent in his daily devotion to God through prayer.

For your leadership to stand the test of time, you need to be consistent in that it doesn't really matter who the decision will affect but that you stand by the same principles for all people and at all times.

Some of the areas that you need to be consistent at include;

- **Decisions** - Our decisions should be void of influence from our relationships, faith affiliations, skin colour or any other consideration that may result in a bias of any kind.

- **Actions** - Are our actions predictable or do we vary depending on our mood. Do we behave differently when happy and when unhappy?

- **Treatment of our followers** - The people you are leading need to see your consistency in recruitment, training and development, remuneration or whatever else concerns them.

CREDIBILITY

This is a very elusive ingredient in the leadership of many yet so crucial for the success of organizations, ministries and churches. It's all about being trustworthy and believable.

You must be the leader who will be known for doing what they say they will do when they say they will do it. It involves honesty, openness and justice in dealing with people.

Many leaders can easily fail the credibility test because it has to do with perception; how people look at our leadership. If you listen to many people in Kenya talk about politicians, they describe them as corrupt, untrustworthy, self-seeking, the list is endless. That means our politicians fail the credibility test. The most unfortunate thing is that there are many honest, faithful and transparent politicians but their credibility has waned over time due to negative perception of the public.

Our credibility can easily be taken away by how we handle finances, relationships and all resources entrusted to us.

Credibility is developed with time and as your followers get to know you better. You will attain credibility if you are first and foremost committed and consistent.

Jesus developed his credibility such that even the centurion who was at the cross when He died proclaimed that Jesus was truly a righteous man. One of the thieves who was crucified with Him confessed that Jesus was truly the Son of God.

Our credibility can easily be taken away by how we handle finances, relationships and all resources entrusted to us.

A saying that has encouraged me to press on is 'winners never quit and quitters never win.' You will not win the leadership challenge by quitting. One of the best tests of true leadership is perseverance and endurance.

Apostle Paul writes to say, *I have fought the good fight, and I have kept the faith and won the race (2 Timothy 4:7)*.

Every game has its rules that you have to subscribe to and abide with in order to win. If you were to play soccer in a field, you must observe the laid out rules or else you will get a yellow card 'warning' to let you know that you are not doing well or even worse get a "red card" disqualifying you from participating in the game all together.

In the event that we are not very careful, we may already have received a 'yellow card' and if we do not tread cautiously, we may be knocked off our leadership responsibilities.

My encouragement to you is that you are walking a path where others have trodden before and made it. He who called and begun a good work in you will be faithful to complete this good work to the glory and honour of His name!

Fulfil your leadership by being committed, consistent and developing credibility.

PRAYER FOR THE LEADER

Father, we thank you for the calling to leadership. I pray that you will help every leader to be committed, consistent and credible.

We know that our followers and the world at large are watching our lives keenly. Help us to remain firm in our convictions and commitments. May our leadership be an example to the current and future generations for the glory and honour of your name.

We ask this in Jesus' name.

Amen.

NOTES & REFERENCE LIST

THE LEADERSHIP CHALLENGE

1. www.divorcemag.com/statistics/stasworld/shtml.
2. http://en.wikipedia.org/wiki/enron.
3. Barbara Kellerman, *Bad Leadership: What it is, How it happens, Why it Matters* (Boston, Mass.: Harvard Business School Press, 2004).

UNDERSTANDING LEADERSHIP

1. J. Oswald Sanders, *Spiritual Leadership*, Rev ed. (Chicago: Moody Press, 1994).
2. John C. Maxwell, *Developing the Leader within You* (Nashville: Thomas Nelson, 1993).
3. Calvin Miller, *The Empowered Leader: 10 Keys to Servant Leadership* (Nashville: Broadman & Holman, 1997).
4. Borek, Lovett & Towns, Space The *Good Book on Leadership: Case Studies From The Bible* (Nashville: Broadman & Holman, 2005).
5. Henry and Richard Blackaby, *Spiritual Leadership: Moving People to God's Agenda* (Nashville: Broadman & Holman, 2001).
6. Ulrich, Zenger & Smallwood, *Results Based Leadership* (Boston, Mass.: Harvard Business School Press, 1999).
7. Jim Zablonski, *The 25 Most Common Problems in Business and How Jesus Solved Them* (Nashville: Broadman & Holman, 1996).

8. Barbara Kellerman, *Bad Leadership: What it is, How it happens, Why it Matters* (Boston, Mass.: Harvard Business School Press, 2004)

Leadership is a Calling

1. Briner and Pritchard, *Leadership Lessons of Jesus* (New York: Gramercy Books, 2001).
2. Hans Finzel, *Top Ten Mistakes Leaders Make* (Colorado Springs: Cook Communications, 2004).
3. Rick Warren, *The Purpose Driven Life: What on earth I am I here for?* (Grand Rapids, Mich.: Zondervan, 2002).
4. Anthony D'Souza, *Being a Leader* (Ghana: African Christian Press, 1990).
5. Wayde Goodall, *Why Great Men Fall* (Green Forest, AR.: New Leaf Press, 2005).
6. George Barna, *Leaders on Leadership: Wisdom, Advice and Encouragement on the Art of Leading God's People* (Ventura, Calif.: Regal Books, 1998).

LEADERSHIP NEEDS PREPARATION

1. John C. Maxwell, *Developing the Leader within You* (Nashville: Thomas Nelson, 1993).
2. J. Robert Clinton, *The Making of a Leader* (Colorado Springs: Navpress, 1988).
3. Rick Warren, *The Purpose Driven Life: What on earth I am I here for?* (Grand Rapids, Mich.: Zondervan, 2002).

LEADERSHIP IS CHARACTER

1. Tom Marshall, *Understanding Leadership* (Grand Rapids: Baker Books, 2003).
2. David Kadalie, *Leader's Resource Kit: Tools and Techniques to Develop your Leadership* (Nairobi, Kenya: Evangel Pub. House, 2006).

3. Max DePree, *Leadership Is an Art* (New York: Dell Publishing, 1989).

4. Charles E. Watson, *What Smart People Do When Dumb Things Happens at Work* (Jaico Publishing House, 2005).

5. Henry and Richard Blackaby, *Spiritual Leadership: Moving People to God's Agenda* (Nashville: Broadman & Holman, 2001).

6. Jack W. Hayford, 'The *Character of a Leader'* cited in *Leaders on Leadership: Wisdom, Advice and Encouragement on the Art of Leading God's People* (Ventura, Calif.: Regal Books, 1998).

7. George Barna, *Leaders on Leadership: Wisdom, Advice and Encouragement on the Art of Leading God's People* (Ventura, Calif.: Regal Books, 1998).

8. Wayde Goodall, *Why Great Men Fall* (Green Forest, AR.: New Leaf Press, 2005).

SUCCESSFUL LEADERS DEPEND ON GOD

1. Henry and Richard Blackaby, *Spiritual Leadership: Moving People to God's Agenda* (Nashville: Broadman & Holman, 2001).

2. Peter Drucker, *The Effective Executive in The Executive in Action* (New York: HarperBusiness, 1996).

3. David Wilkerson, *The Salvation of your face: You need a Holy Ghost face-Lift!* (New York: Times Square pulpit Series, 1995).

LEADERSHIP REQUIRES COURAGE

1. Wayde Goodall, *Why Great Men Fall* (Green Forest, AR.: New Leaf Press, 2005).

2. Charles E. Watson, *What Smart People Do When Dumb Things Happens at Work* (Jaico Publishing House, 2005).

3. J. Oswald Sanders, *Spiritual Leadership*, Rev ed. (Chicago: Moody Press, 1994).

4. Calvin Miller, *The Empowered Leader: 10 Keys to Servant Leadership* (Nashville: Broadman & Holman, 1997).

5. John White, *Excellence in Leadership: Reaching Goals with Prayer, Courage and Determination* (Downers Grove, IL.: InterVarsity Press, 1986).

6. Bill Hybels, *Courageous Leadership* (Nairobi, Kenya: Evangel Pub. House, 2004).

7. David Kadalie, *Leader's Resource Kit: Tools and Techniques to Develop your Leadership* (Nairobi, Kenya: Evangel Pub. House, 2006)

8. Martin Kalungu-Banda, *Leading like Madiba: Lessons of leadership from Nelson Mandela* (Double Storey, 2006).

LEADERS EXPERIENCE CONFLICT

1. McShane & Von Glinow, *Organizational Behaviour* (New York, USA: Mc-Grawhill, 2005).

2. Ed Rowell, *Go the Distance* (Nairobi, Kenya: Evangel Pub. House, 2006).

3. Jim Van Yperen, 'The Refining Fire of Leadership' cited on *Leaders on Lead-ership: Wisdom, Advice and Encouragement on the Art of Leading God's People* (Ventura, Calif.: Regal Books, 1998).

4. David Johnson and Roger Johnson, *Reducing School Violence through Conflict Resolution* (Association for Supervision & Curriculum Deve, 1995).

LEADERSHIP IS COMMUNICATION

1. Max DePree, *Leadership Is an Art* (New York: Dell Publishing, 1989).

2. Wayde Goodall, *Why Great Men Fall* (Green Forest, AR.: New Leaf Press, 2005).

NOTES & REFERENCE LIST

3. Benjamin Kaufman, *'Pressing on! Why Leaders Derail and What to do About it'* cited on *Why Great Men Fall* (Green Forest, AR.: New Leaf Press, 2005).

AGE IS JUST BUT A NUMBER

1. Charles E. Watson, *What Smart People Do When Dumb Things Happens at Work* (Jaico Publishing House, 2005).
2. Barbara Kellerman, *Bad Leadership: What it is, How it happens, Why it Matters* (Boston, Mass.: Harvard Business School Press, 2004).

APPENDICES

APPENDIX A: VARIOUS DEFINITIONS OF LEADERSHIP

- "leadership is like the Abominable Snowman, whose footprints are everywhere but who is nowhere to be seen" *Bennis & Nanus: 'Leaders: Strategies for Taking Charge'* (1997)
- "Moving people on to God's agenda." *(Henry & Richard Blackaby, Spiritual Leadership)*
- "[There are] almost as many definitions of leadership as there are persons who have attempted to define the concept." *Stogdill* (1974, p.259)
- "A leader is a dealer in hope." *Napoleon Bonaparte*, French soldier, statesman, revolutionary (1769-1821)
- "A leader is best when people barely know that he exists, not so good when people obey and acclaim him, worst when they despise him. 'Fail to honor people' they fail to honor you.' But of a good leader, who talks little, when his work is done, his aim fulfilled, they will all say, 'We did this ourselves.'" *Lao Tzu*, Chinese founder of Taoism, author (6th Century BC)
- "A leader shapes and shares a vision which gives point to the work of others." *Charles Handy* (1992)
- "A leader takes people where they want to go. A great leader takes people where they don't necessarily want to go, but ought to be." *Rosalynn Carter*, US First Lady (b.1927)

- "As we look ahead into the next century, leaders will be those who empower others." *Bill Gates*

- "Be willing to make decisions. That's the most important quality in a good leader." *General George S. Patton Jr.*

- "Leaders are individuals who establish direction for a working group of individuals who gain commitment from these group of members to this direction and who then motivate these members to achieve the direction's outcomes." *Conger, J. A. 'Learning to Lead' San Francisco: Jossey Bass (1992, p18)*

- "Leaders are those who consistently make effective contributions to social order, and who are expected and perceived to do so." *Hosking (1988, p.153)*

- "Leadership (according to John Sculley) revolves around vision, ideas, direction, and has more to do with inspiring people as to direction and goals than with day-to-day implementation. A leader must be able to leverage more than his own capabilities. He must be capable of inspiring other people to do things without actually sitting on top of them with a checklist." *Bennis, W.' On Becoming a Leader' Reading, MA: Addison-Wesley Publishing, (1989, p.139)*

- "Leadership and learning are indispensable to each other." *John F. Kennedy*

- "Leadership is a combination of strategy and character. If you must be without one, be without the strategy." *Gen. H. Norman Schwarzkopf*

- "Leadership is a development of a clear and complete system of expectations in order to identify, evoke and use the strengths of all resources in the organization the most important of which is people." *Batten, J. D. 'Tough Minded Leadership' New York: AMACOM (1989 p. 35)*

- "Leadership is a function of knowing yourself, having a vision that is well communicated, building trust among colleagues, and taking effective action to realize your own leadership potential." *Warren Bennis*

- "Leadership is a process of giving purpose (meaningful direction) to collective effort, and causing willing effort to be expended to achieve purpose." *Jacobs & Jaques* (1990, p.281)

- "Leadership is a process of influence between a leader and those who are followers." *Hollander* (1978, p.1)

- "Leadership is a process whereby an individual influences a group of individuals to achieve a common goal." *Northouse* (2004, p.3)

- "Leadership is an attempt at influencing the activities of followers through the communication process and toward the attainment of some goal or goals." *Donelly, J.H. & Ivancevich, J. M. & Gibson, J.L. 'Organizations: behavior, structure, processes 5th Ed.' Plano, TX: Business Publications Inc. (1985 p.362).*

- "Leadership is an influence process that enable managers to get their people to do willingly what must be done, do well what ought to be done." *Cribbin, J.J. 'Leadership: strategies for organizational effectiveness' New York: AMACOM (1981).*

- "Leadership is defined as the process of influencing the activities of an organized group toward goal achievement." *Rauch & Behling* (1984, p.46)

- "Leadership is discovering the company's destiny and having the courage to follow it." *Joe Jaworski* - Organizational Learning Center at MIT.

- "Leadership is influence – nothing more, nothing less." *John Maxwell*, 1998

- "Leadership is interpersonal influence, exercised in a situation, and directed, through the communication process, toward the attainment of a specified goal or goals." *Tannenbaum, Weschler & Massarik* (1961, p.24)

- "Leadership is not a person or a position. It is a complex moral relationship between people, based on trust, obligation, commitment, emotion, and a shared vision of the good." *Joanne Ciulla* (1998)

- "Leadership is that process in which one person sets the purpose or direction for one or more other persons and gets them to move along together with him or her and with each other in that direction with competence and full commitment." *Jaques E. & Clement, S.D.* 'Executive Leadership: A practical guide to managing complexity' Cambridge, MA: Carson-Hall & Co. Publishers (1994, p.4)

- "Leadership is the accomplishment of a goal through the direction of human assistants. A leader is one who successfully marshals his human collaborators to achieve particular ends." *Prentice, W.C.H.* 'Understanding Leadership' Harvard Business Review September/October 1961 vol. 39 no. 5 p.143.

- "Leadership is the art of influencing others to their maximum performance to accomplish any task, objective or project." *Cohen, W.A.* 'The Art of a Leader' Englewood Cliffs, NJ: Prentice Hall (1990, p. 9).

- "Leadership is the art of mobilizing others to want to struggle for shared aspirations." *Kouzes, J.M. & Posner, B.Z.* 'The Leadership Challenge' San Francisco: Jossey-Bass (1995, p.30).

- "Leadership is the behavior of an individual when he is directing the activities of a group toward a shared goal." *Hemphill & Coons* (1957, p.7)

- "Leadership is the capacity to translate vision into reality." *Warren G. Bennis.*

- "Leadership is the incremental influence that a person has beyond his or her formal authority." (Vecchio, 1988).

- "Leadership is the influential increment over and above mechanical compliance with the routine directives of the organization." *Katz & Kahn* (1978, p. 528)

- "Leadership is the initiation and maintenance of structure in expectation and interaction." *Stogdill* (1974, p.411)

- "Leadership may be considered as the process (act) of influencing the activities of an organized group in its efforts toward goal setting and goal achievement." *Stogdill,* (1950, p.3)

- "Leadership requires using power to influence the thoughts and actions of other people." *Zalenik, A.* 'Managers and Leaders: are they different?' Harvard Business Review March/ April 1992 p.126.

- "Management is efficiency in climbing the ladder of success; leadership determines whether the ladder is leaning against the right wall." *Stephen R. Covey*

- "People ask the difference between a leader and a boss....The leader works in the open, and the boss in covert. The leader leads, and the boss drives." *Theodore Roosevelt*

- "The final test of a leader is that he leaves behind in others the conviction and will to carry on." *Walter Lippman*

- "The first responsibility of a leader is to define reality. The last is to say thank you. In between the two, the leader must become a servant and a debtor. That sums up the progress of an artful leader." *Max DePree*

- "The function of leadership is to produce more leaders, not more followers." *Ralph Nadar*

- "The growth and development of people is the highest calling of leadership." *Harvey S. Firestone*

- "The job of the leader is to speak to the possibility." *Benjamin Zander,* British conductor, management presenter (b.1939)

- "The key to successful leadership today is influence, not authority." *Kenneth Blanchard,* US management author, presenter (b.1939)

- "The only definition of a leader is someone who has followers." *The Drucker Foundation,* 1996

- "You manage things, you lead people." *Admiral Grace Murray Hooper,* US naval officer (1906-1992)

- "A leader is the person in a group who directs and coordinates task-oriented group activities." *Fiedler (1967)*

- "Leaders are those who consistently make effective contributions to social order and who are expected and perceived to do so." *Hosking (1988)*

- "Leadership is a social process in which one individual influences the behaviour of others without the use of threat or violence." *Buchannan and Huczynski (1997, p.606)*

- "Leadership is about articulating visions, embodying values, and creating the environment within which things can be accomplished." *Richards and Engle (1986)*

- "Leadership is the ability to step outside the culture to start evolutionary change processes that are more adaptive." *Schein (1992)*

- "Leadership is the creation of a vision about a desired future state which seeks to enmesh all members of an organization in its net." *Bryman (1986, p. 6)*

- "Leadership is the lifting of a man's vision to higher sights, the raising of a man's performance to a higher standard, the building of a man's personality beyond its normal limitations." *Drucker, P. F. (1955)*

- "Leadership is the process of influencing the activities of an individual or a group in efforts toward goal achievement in a given situation." *Hersey, P. & Blanchard, K. 'Management of Organizational Behavior'. Englewood Cliffs, NJ: Prentice Hall (1988 p. 86)*

- "Leadership is the process of making sense of what people are doing together so that people will understand and be committed." *Drath & Palus (1994)*

- "Leadership: the art of getting someone else to do something you want done because he wants to do it." *Dwight D Eisenhower (1890 -1969) US Statesman*

- "One of the hardest tasks of leadership is understanding that you are not what you are, but what you're perceived to be by others." *Edward*

L. Flom, CEO of the Florida Steel Corporation, in a speech, May 6, 1987.

- "Leadership is all hype. We've had three great leaders in this century – Hitler, Stalin and Mao." *Peter Drucker,* quoted in Fortune, 21/02/94
- "Leadership is an intangible quality with no clear definition. That's probably a good thing ,because if the people who were being led knew the definition, they would hunt down their leaders and kill them." *Scott Adams,* The Dilbert Principle (1996)
- "Leadership: The capacity and will to rally people to a common purpose together with the character that inspires confidence and trust" *Field Marshal Montgomery*
- "A Leader: A person responsible for achieving objectives through others by creating the conditions in which they may be successful and for building and maintaining the team that he or she is a member of." *Jeremy Tozer*
- "Leadership is a purposeful relationship, which occurs episodically among participants, who use their individual skills in influence, to advocate transforming change." *Michael S. Kearns,* 2005
- "Leadership is an influence relationship among leaders and followers who intend real changes that reflect their mutual purposes." *Joseph Rost,* Leadership in the 21st Century, (1993, p.102)

SOME OTHER DEFINITIONS OF LEADERSHIP INCLUDE:

- My definition of a leader . . . is a man who can persuade people to do what they don't want to do, or do what they're too lazy to do, and like it. *Harry S. Truman,* 1884-1972, Thirty-third President of the United States, Miller, More Plan Speaking
- You cannot manage men into battle. You manage things; you lead people. *Grace Hopper,* Admiral, U. S. Navy (retired), Nova (PBS TV), 1986

- The superior leader gets things done with very little motion. He imparts instruction not through many words but through a few deeds. He keeps informed about everything but interferes hardly at all. He is a catalyst, and though things would not get done well if he weren't there, when they succeed he takes no credit. And because he takes no credit, credit never leaves him. *Lao Tse, Tao Te Ching*

- Leadership occurs when one person induces others to work toward some predetermined objectives. *Massie*

- Leadership is the ability of a superior to influence the behavior of a subordinate or group and persuade them to follow a particular course of action. *Chester Bernard*

- Leadership is the art to of influencing and directing people in such a way that will win their obedience, confidence, respect and loyal cooperation in achieving common objectives. *US Air Force*

- Be gentle and you can be bold; be frugal and you can be liberal; avoid putting yourself before others and you can become a leader among men. *Lao Tze*

- The first job of a leader is to define a vision for the organization ... Leadership of the capacity to translate vision into reality. *Warren Bennis, President, University of Cincinnati, University of Maryland symposium, January 21, 1988*

- The ultimate test of practical leadership is the realization of intended, real change that meets people's enduring needs. *James MacGregor Burns.*

- Managers have subordinates—leaders have followers. *Murray Johannsen*

- Leadership is the possession of certain key character qualities essential for achieving positive holistic change. These qualities are made manifest once an individual becomes accountable to a group through a position of responsibility that involves the opportunity for transformation. *Kirk Kauffeldt, 2005*

APPENDIX B: CHARACTER QUALITIES

Character is grounded in integrity, and reinforced by balancing Equity (a sense of partnership and equality) and Responsibility (the accountability and action-orientation that gets things done). This is clearly illustrated by the table on the following page with character qualities downloaded from www.southerninstitute.org.

Overarching Elements	Qualities	Leadership Character	Organizational Character
Integrity		Basic Integrity – defined by honesty, authenticity, and truth telling – is the foundation for being seen as an ethical leader.	Basic Integrity – defined by honesty, authenticity, and truth telling – is the foundation for an ethical organization.
Equity	Respect	Treating everyone in the organization with respect helps leaders earn trust. Leaders who are respectful to everyone are seen as less "political."	An organization high in respect treats everyone, employees and customers alike, as valued members of the organization community
	Self Confidence	Leaders with self-confidence are less likely to go along with the crowd, and feel confident and assertive enough to speak their minds.	An organization with confidence is proud of its accomplishments and its culture, and feels that it can win in the marketplace.
	Humility	Humility keeps leaders from appearing arrogant or self-righteous, and keeps the ethical conversation open.	Willing to learn from other organizations, open to change and the need to change, not too proud to look inward.
	Emotional Mastery	Leaders who are explosive are viewed as lacking in empathy and consideration for others, and don't hear the truth in the organization.	The norms of the organization support constructive conflict and openness, but don't support explosiveness and hostility.
Responsibility	Accountability	Leaders who are accountable follow through on commitments and are willing to hold other people accountable.	Accountable organizations get results, keep promises to customers, and stay focused on goals.
	Lack of Blame	People who project blame are seen as irresponsible and lacking in integrity.	In organizations high in this quality, departments don't blame each other and take responsibility when things go wrong.
	Courage	Leaders with courage are willing to address uncomfortable issues and take risk, even when they may endanger their own position or career.	Organizations with courage own up to mistakes, make reparations quickly, take risks, and try new things readily.
	Focus on the Whole	Leaders who focus on the whole are able to put the organization's interest or even the larger community's interest above their own self-interest or their own department's interest.	An organization that promotes a focus on the whole shares information widely and helps everyone understand how they work together to make the whole successful.

ABOUT THE AUTHOR

Kirimi Barine is an author, trainer, publisher and consultant. He has served and continues to serve in various leadership capacities for organizations in Africa and around the world.

He is an author of several books among them Rediscovering Leadership: Principles to launch and grow your leadership, Successful Leadership: 8 essential principles that you must know, Transformational Leadership in the Local Church, A training manual for the Transformational Church Leadership program of PAC University, and co-authored Transformational Corporate Leadership, Leading Strategic Change, A Life Well Lived: living to leave a Legacy, USA and The Kenya National Anthem: Our prayer & heritage. He has also developed a leadership Curriculum Leadership Foundations with three modules, Leading from the Heart, Leading with your Head and Leading with your Hands as well as contributing articles to various magazines around the world.

Barine is a holder of a Doctor of Philosophy (PhD) in Business Administration (Leadership & Governance) from the Central University of Nicaragua and a Doctorate degree in Business Administration at SMC University in Switzerland. His research and Dissertation was in the area of Governance and Leadership in private Universities in Kenya. He holds a Masters degree in Business Administration (MBA) and a Bachelor of Education degree from Kenyatta and Egerton Universities respectively. His research, teaching and consulting mainly focuses on Leadership, Governance, Organizational Behaviour, Strategic Leadership and Management.

Barine enjoys continuous learning and hence teaches Leadership and Governance at St. Paul's University as an adjunct faculty member in the MBA & BALM programs. In addition, he has supervised students doing their Research Projects and enjoys training and facilitation in seminars as well as consultancy related assignments. He has had wide opportunities to serve and consult on leadership both in Kenya and around the world.

The author would appreciate your comments.

Contact him through:

kirimi.barine@gmail.com

Other Books by the same Author

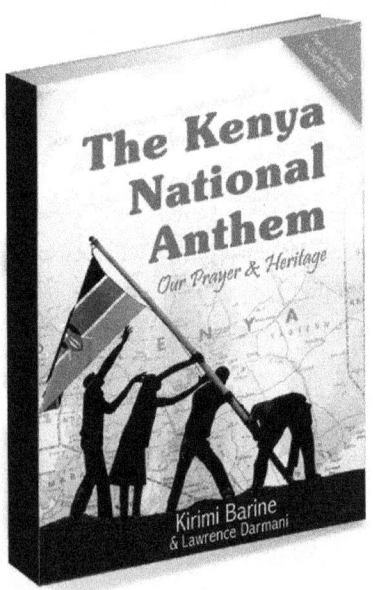

OTHER BOOKS BY THE SAME AUTHOR

www.ingramcontent.com/pod-product-compliance
Lightning Source LLC
Chambersburg PA
CBHW032357040426
42451CB00006B/43